WISH YOU WERE HERE

ENGLAND ON SEA

Also by Travis Elborough

The Bus We Loved: London's Affair with the Routemaster

The Long-Player Goodbye:
The Album from Vinyl to iPod and Back Again

WISH YOU WERE HERE

ENGLAND ON SEA

TRAVIS ELBOROUGH

SCEPTRE

First published in Great Britain in 2010 by Sceptre
An imprint of Hodder & Stoughton
An Hachette UK company

1

Copyright © Travis Elborough 2010

The right of Travis Elborough to be identified as the Author of the Work has been
asserted by him in accordance with the Copyright, Designs and Patents Act 1988.

A CIP catalogue record for this title is available from the British Library.

ISBN 978 0 340 935101

Typeset in Sabon by Hewer Text UK Ltd, Edinburgh
Printed and bound in the UK by Clays Ltd

Hodder & Stoughton policy is to use papers that are natural, renewable
and recyclable products and made from wood grown in sustainable
forests. The logging and manufacturing processes are expected to
conform to the environmental regulations of the country of origin.

Hodder & Stoughton Ltd
338 Euston Road
London NW1 3BH

www.hodder.co.uk

For George and Joan

Contents

Introduction

Figuratively Speaking – The Seaside as a Prelapsarian Realm – Pirate-Themed Eateries and the Obligatory Autobiographical Bit – The Staycation Nation – The Same Old Excuses for What Follows

When you think about it, the metaphors are not encouraging. Figuratively speaking, to be 'at sea' is to be lost, confused or lacking knowledge and competence. Ditto for 'adrift'. On dry land it is a pejorative that reeks of purposelessness and the absence of guidance or intention. 'Beached', while describing a physical condition suffered by oil tankers, seals and whales, can be deployed for any moment of stranded helplessness. Or even abandonment and death. And consulting the nearest dictionary to hand for the phrase 'washed up', I find, 'informal: no longer effective or successful'. A definition that, though accurate, seems too mechanistic and skimps on all the emotive, associative images with alcoholism and those pickled former West End or Hollywood stars dowsing their grapefruit in vodka each sunup. The type whose days end in floods of tears and gin; spider's legs of mascara scampering down now ravished 'Faces of 1929' as they contemplate their long-vanished fame in ever advancing states of infirmity, forgetfulness and inebriation. And, as often as not, in coastal bungalows or seaside retirement homes. In ancient Greek mythology, after all, the aquatic and alcoholic were often conjoined; Dionysus, the god of wine, transforms a band of Tyrrhenian pirates into dolphins after foiling their attempt to sell him into slavery. And for Homer in *The Iliad* and *The Odyssey*, the sea is frequently 'wine dark'.

So if the oceans are to be plundered for anything in the English language, it is largely as fonts of negative imagery. For every 'shipshape' and 'sailing by' there is a 'sunk', 'marooned', 'out of your depth' or 'wrecked'. This pessimism may or may not be a direct result of Great Britain possessing some 11,072.76 miles of damp, frequently unforgiving coastline and a climate that swathes everything in drear halftones for large parts of the year. But that coastline and that weather are the things that define us above all else.

As Jonathan Raban notes in the *Oxford Book of the Sea*, to leave these isles is to go 'overseas'. Whether the occupants of this island are by dint of their curious, mongrel genetic inheritance simply naturally predisposed to view the world, and by extension that coastline and that weather, in purely glass half-empty terms, continues to be a matter of debate. (At least, among tanked-up barroom philosophers in draughty, badly lit pubs discoursing over beers on long, rain-lashed, winter evenings, anyway.)

What is not up for argument, however, is that the English are, by and large, a nation of Eeyores. The mere existence of A.A. Milne's Eeyore, possibly the most maudlin but best loved character in the annals of children's literature, speaks volumes about the national psyche. Any country that can take a pessimistic toy donkey that lives in a corner of 100 Acre Wood called 'the Gloomy Place', so eagerly to its hearts is unlikely to possess the cheeriest of dispositions.[1] But then, being pessimistic is not quite the same as being unhappy. It is something of a cliché that the English are never happier than when complaining. And up until fairly recently, complaining about our seaside towns, once one of

---

1 Traditionally donkeys are usually figures of foolishness in stories, fables and soundbites about the First World War, stupid and/or naughty rather than dour, haughty and convinced of their superior intellect. A factor that surely only adds to Eeyore's appeal. And once the thrill of childhood beach rides is over, who has not felt that donkeys look rather forlorn at the seaside, locked into their Sisyphean treks back and forth along the sands?

the few spheres in the land given almost solely over to fun, had been close to a national sport. A sport where there was an almost perverse pleasure or pride, perhaps, in gloating over their apparent awfulness.

Bill Cormack wrote in his 1998 book *A History of Holidays: 1812-1990*, that 'the high summer of the English holiday resort is over. Some have deteriorated so much that they have become vulgar, almost squalid. Even day-trippers have deserted them.' Few, in all honesty, would probably have disagreed with him then. Nor disputed his claim that when contrasted with the holidaying attractions of Spain, where it 'always seems warm and sunny even in November' and 'drink went on until the small hours', indigenous resorts had a tricky job on their hands.

Publishing its first survey of Britain's 'Crap Towns' in 2003, the *Idler* magazine placed three resorts (Morecambe, Bexhill and Hythe) in its 'top' ten. A further four (Brighton, Aldeburgh, Hayling Island and Hastings) had 'respectable' rankings in the full list of fifty. It hardly a serious exercise and frequently just plain rude, the presence of so many resorts in a comic roll call of national shame that included Cumbernauld, the concrete Scottish new town widely derided as an atrocity of post-war planning, was indicative enough all the same.

Even in a recent film about the life of the record producer Joe Meek, coastal gigs are virtually synonymous with failure. 'He's got me doing all these seaside towns,' a disgruntled Heinz Burt spits at Meek in one scene. J.J. Feild, playing the Southampton bacon slicer turned platinum blonde rocker and Arthur Askey-supporting summer seasoner, rings every ounce of fury out of those last two words. Elsewhere in the picture it is implied that the creation of the chart-topping 1962 hit 'Telstar' that lends the movie its name, was nearly derailed by Tornados drummer Clem Cattini's insistence on fulfilling a booking in Great Yarmouth. And all this from men responsible for 'Blackpool Rock' and 'The Ice Cream Man' – a pair of echo-laden instrumentals stuffed with the usual Meek studio gimcracks that trill with the same plaintive urgency as the chimes on a Stop Me And Buy One van. If not the maudlin and rather marshal ching-a-ling of a fairground Merry-Go-Round organ to boot. And for all of its associations with the out of this world, there was always a touch of the Tower Ballroom Wurlitzer about the Clavioline keyboard Meek used on many of his arrangements. But then the film is pandering to received ideas about seaside resorts as decrepit, and potent emblems of decay, for comic and dramatic effect. These ideas, and their realities for that matter, were far less advanced in Meek's day than our own.

At the Festival of Britain in 1951, an event staged to persuade the world that the country was back on its feet after the war, a replica seafront joined such thrusting totems of modernity as the Skylon, on London's South Bank. As an entry for the exhibit in the Festival's guidebook helpfully explained, 'Whenever the British feel the need to relax – either after a heavy week in their industrial cities or a hard year on the land – they tend to head to the sea.' Written in English by Ian Cox, its words were obviously intended for the benefit of foreign visitors who'd mastered the language but remained somewhat perplexed about national customs. Further on, Cox maintains that every stick of lettered seaside rock, a confection that dates back to the 1870s at the earliest, 'contains an ancient mystery' – a conundrum on a par, presumably, with the riddle in the sands or the standing stones at Stonehenge. (Though with sweets only just 'off the ration' at that point, where these supplies of rock came from might possibly have presented a bigger mystery to festival-goers.) More compellingly, he goes on to define a 'characteristically British' seafront. In his view, it is 'a medley of Victorian boarding houses, elegant bow-fronted Regency facades, ice-cream parlours, pubs, and the full and friendly gaudiness of the amusement park.'

Over half a century later, this description of British seafront-ery still sounds compellingly attractive. Cox, quoting from an old music hall number, also noted that 'We do a lot of things at the seaside that we can't do in town.' The song in question, 'You Can Do A Lot of Things at the Seaside' turns on the faintly salacious comic motif of respectable mothers stripping off and paddling as they might at the beach, in the fountains of Trafalgar Square. (It's Edwardian. I guess, you took your jollies where you could back then.) But the quote and the original song acknowledged liberties at the seaside that even by 1951 hardly prevailed elsewhere in England. Though enormously circumscribed by ritual and only validated by being under-taken en masse, here, was one of the rare spaces in English life where you were actively encouraged to let yourself go. So long as you didn't let yourself down, naturally.

Endlessly recycled Pathé news footage and stills from the *Picture Post* of the period capture what now seem almost unfeasibly large crowds of people of all shapes and sizes and all ages communing on the sands and shingle at Blackpool, Brighton, Margate, Southend, Great Yarmouth, Clacton, Bournemouth et al. Old men in flat caps and three-piece suits with rolled up trousers paddle in the shallows. Plump grannies in flowery frocks doze in striped deckchairs beside buxom Jayne Mansfield-types in sunglasses and strappy tops reading magazines. Pipe-smoking dads with odd cliffs of hair supervise boys in saggy knitted swimming trunks with wooden model ships and little girls with buckets and spades. Smudgers in blazers armed with spider monkeys and cameras like ribs of meat, prowl the esplanades. Salvation Army bands, sweat cresting the brows beneath their caps oompah their way through moral stiffening tunes. And so on and so on.

These kind of images, though almost ancient history now, feel so instantly recognizable, such a part of England's collective consciousnesses, our folk memory, they could almost have been arc welded into the back of our retinas. Dubious dentistry, tonsorial misdemeanours and the almost overwhelming pastiness of complexions aside, they serve to conjure up a rather idyllic and seductive image of the English seaside in its prime. Everyone in these films or photographs seems content and is busy getting on with the job of relaxing and enjoying themselves. Whatever social differences there were, and there were no doubt many, appear to have been washed away by the salt water or bleached out by the sun. Rather like the NHS, the beach here is one of the great English egalitarian institutions, open to everyone and near enough free at the point of entry.

Places where differences are tolerated and eccentricities positively encouraged, beaches also seem to represent those facets of the English character that we still cherish most of all. (Or the most agreeable facets of ourselves that we choose to elevate to national characteristics, i.e., our level headedness, our sense of fair play, our stoicism, our anti-authoritarianism, our respect for individuality, our distrust of showy displays of intelligence or wealth, etc., etc.) As such and beyond mere post-war national propaganda, the seaside is easy to imbue with a mythic significance. Its allure is visceral – we are an island after all – but also deeply cultural. And from today's perspective and with our knowledge of their subsequent fate, resorts from the 1950s have the look of a prelapsarian realm. Since most of us first encounter the seaside as children this is arguably not so surprising. Perhaps, in a sense, every trip to the beach as an adult is an attempt to recapture lost innocence or at least to feel as carefree as a child. And the urge to inflict the experience on our own children, if we have any, is both a baton-handing exercise and a chance to sample those moments again, vicariously.

In terms of form meeting function, though, the English seaside really did reach a kind of peak in the 1950s. By then, legislation entitling the nation's workforce to holi days with pay, passed just before the war but only coming into full effect afterwards, was providing the majority of Britons with the means to take a proper break. For most, a holiday meant a trip to the seaside, plain and simple. The two terms, for millions at this point and for a decade or so yet, remained virtually indistinguishable.

After the ravages and uncertainties of the conflict, the seaside, with that medley of Victorian boarding houses, Regency facades, ice-cream parlours, pubs and gaudy amusement parks et al., were a comfortingly homely sight. As John Betjeman had suggested in his poem 'Margate, 1940', coastal resorts were 'the fairy-light sights' of England that we'd been 'fighting for, foremost of all'. To visit the seaside and waddle along the deck of a pier in peacetime was to perform a sort of victory salute, if you like. The pleasure of gazing out to sea heightened, surely, by the knowledge that the land behind you was safe and secure, at least for the time being and no enemy aggressors lurked beyond the mist in the distance.

With austerity slowly giving way to affluence, and the population in full employment becoming keener and keener on having a good time but left with few alternatives to a domestic holiday, the English seaside enjoyed a golden era of prosperity. But newly affordable consumer goods and a huge increase in the ownership of cars and televisions would soon enough reconfigure attitudes towards luxury, leisure and travel. Increasing self-sufficiency in terms of transport brought with it a greater promiscuity when it came to holidaying destinations. Those who didn't abandon the seaside entirely – or even England, on cheap package deals to Spain – were more frequently to be discovered nesting in outlying caravan parks and camping sites.

And in the white heat of this go-getting technological age, a period when Doric arches were bulldozed in the name of progress and modernist shopping centres, beached spaceports in concrete and glass, materialised up and down the land, a trip to the seaside would start to feel ever more like going back in time. Their rickety Victorian piers, crumbling music hall theatres, rusting bandstands and rotting beach huts were viewed as museum pieces; diversions that only the terminally nostalgic, mentally deficient or wilfully perverse could in all seriousness entertain over other options.

Or certainly that was how it still seemed, when I was

growing up by the seaside in the 1970s and 80s. Brighton
may very probably have rocked. It had *Quadrophenia* and
The Piranhas. But Worthing?

Later Suede might well have equated the town with the
next life but it was hard to come of age in a place where
almost everyone else has gone to die. Or those who haven't
are merely passing through seeking temporary oblivion in
slot machines, ice creams and lazy sunny afternoons.

It was not impossible, obviously. Nor, in retrospect, especially terrible, really. But it was to spend formative years at
what felt like the wrong end of the line: biologically, chron-
ologically and geographically. Any town where the most
urgent appointment of any week for the bulk of its inhabitants is with a post office counter is bound to suffer from a
degree of lethargy. And as a child, inactivity, immobility, is
just much more unbearable. Rather like being trapped on a
planet with a different gravitational field, every action was
so heavily weighted against you.

The general tendency toward rest, in any case, certainly
appeared to adhere to what little I'd grasped then of
Newtonian physics.[2] A cursory scan of the buildings on
the front, stucco peeling and stained yellowish like smok-
ers' teeth or concrete, mottled and greying, seemed to show
that the Second Law of Thermodynamics – at least as
expressed by Woody Allen – was having a whale of a time.[3]

2 Though as any peregrinations along the promenade seemed to be accompanied
  by almost constant chewing, all those loose false teeth bovinely grinding away
  on Murray mints, figuring out the necessary coefficients to calculate motion, let
  alone the resistance, would always have proved far beyond me.
3 At one point in *Husbands and Wives*, Allen claims, 'It's the Second Law of
  Thermodynamics: sooner or later everything turns to shit.'

Although time itself was not so much relative as retrograde. In a scene worthy of Monty Python's *Holy Grail*, I dimly recall, a tarot card reader was accused of witchcraft by local campaigners and eventually forced from their booth on the pier. Python's *Life of Brian*, deemed blasphemous, was effectively banned.

As a former resident who'd had the good taste to slip the town's name into an exceedingly witty play, the safely dead Oscar Wilde might just about be forgiven for his sexual leanings. Though any trace of his presence in the town was eradicated when the Esplanade Hotel where he wrote *The Importance of Being Earnest* was demolished to build a petrol station in the 1960s. But here in droves were the ageing bigots whose narrow waists and broad minds, as Wilde once quipped, had long since changed places. In my late teens, it was still possible to come across duffers who proudly boasted that they hadn't been to Brighton 'in years' because 'nowadays it was full of fuckin' queers.' (What it had been like in Lord Alfred Douglas's prime was scarcely worth pointing out to them.) When it came to race, the situation was arguably worse. Having elected a fascist councillor in the 1930s, fifty years later Worthing was home to the National Front's HQ. Montague Street, the town's main shopping thoroughfare, was prowled by two skinheads who attended my school, and were evidently devoted enough to the cause to spend each Saturday afternoon trying to flog copies of its house organ, *Bulldog*, to passing shoppers. Saner types were out browsing record racks or chasing girls.

It was the endemic smallness and the sheer petty mindedness of the place – and its ilk – that, for me, David Leland's

Wish You Were Here captured with such acuity. This picture was filmed in and around Worthing in 1986 but set in 1951 – a wall mural for the Festival of Britain is shown in one scene. It starred a fifteen-year-old Emily Lloyd as Lynda Mansell, a sexually precocious, if vulnerable teenager, kicking against the pricks in a drearily conservative (and Conservative) seaside town.

Over the course of the film, Lynda has sex with just two men. The first is Dave, a young bus conductor played by Jesse Birdsall, who fancies himself as a bit of a Lothario. In the bedroom, he sports yellow silk pyjamas and smokes Du Maurier cigarettes in a holder but ends up under-mining this self-consciously debonair image by wailing 'any more fares pleeeese' when he comes (prematurely). Having introduced Lynda to condoms and the art of love, he soon betrays her. His duplicity is quickly revealed when he unknowingly cycles up to the seafront fish and chip kiosk where she works with his new redheaded squeeze in tow.

Her next affair is with Eric, a middle-aged friend of her widowed father. The projectionist in the local cinema, The Dome, Eric, rendered arrestingly sinister by Tom Bell, is a rather callous, gaunt boozer with a limp and oily jet-black hair. He is man who you suspect would have perpetually clammy hands and the shakes in those precious seconds when saloon door bolts are yanked back in the seconds up to opening time. Physically crippled, his sexual approaches to Lynda seem fuelled by vengeful, misogynistic anger as much as lust. Though loss of one kind or another, possibly self-esteem and mobility for Eric and, the premature death of her mother for Lynda, binds them together. Claiming to be 'the best bare back rider in town' he refuses to use 'a plonker' and consequently impregnates the teenager.

Leaving aside the rest of the drama for today, what anyone visiting the film's locations will discover is that the bus depot is right behind the cinema. You can just about make this out in the movie itself, though unless you know the buildings, their complete proximity is probably less easy to surmise. But armed with this knowledge, Lynda's circumstances assume an added poignancy. One that hit me with particular force when I saw the film in situ on its release. The paucity of her options is such that both her shags, in effect, spend every working day within a few yards of each other.

Even at what was supposed to be thirty-five years on, the claustrophobia of this tableau, very nearly a *Huis Clos* on sea, seemed to sum up the narrowness of horizons on offer. The most expansive thing around was the ocean itself. Faced with its undulating enormity, it was as if life on land had contracted in overcompensation. To a curious adolescent – and I was curious in every sense of the word – hung up on my own angst, there appeared to be either nothing of interest or a great squally, nothingness whichever direction you looked.

It goes almost without saying that being a resident is nothing like being a visitor. And teenagers are, of course, practically biologically disposed to be dissatisfied with their lot, judging especially harshly surroundings that were once, perhaps, the most comfortingly familiar. Or at least familial. Julian Barnes, reflecting on his relationship with our nearest Continental neighbour once wrote that 'in the long, silent quarrel and faux existentialism of late adolescence', he took against his 'parents' values and therefore against their love of France'. Swap 'seaside' for 'France' and you have my own story, pretty much.

Nothing could be dearer to my parents than living by the sea. While even his beloved Brighton and Hove Albion Football Club ('The Seagulls') were once hauled off to landlocked Gillingham for a season or two, my father has stuck, limpet-like, to a tiny segment of the Sussex coast for his entire life. His sense of place is enviably complete. The sea has remained such a constant that anything else would be unbearable, possibly unimaginable, now. A relocation to Croydon, mooted exceedingly fleetingly at one point in the late 1970s and in relation to some, apparently un-commutable, job opportunity, was vetoed immediately by my mother, largely on grounds that it was 'not by the sea.' This irrefutable fact, informed by her knowledge of the terrain (she was born in Redhill and spent formative years in South Merstham), was enough to settle the issue without the need for further discussion.

This loyalty to the seaside was not restricted to our unit alone. It was a broader trait, practically genetic and not unlike bushy eyebrows, long, sharp noses, a fondness for drink and a relish of talk and dry wit, common to the tribe as a whole. How far back this dates is a matter of some conjecture. The Victorian family branch line includes well-documented stops in the decidedly urban (or then suburban) Lewisham, Kennington and Chalk Farm. By Edwardian times, births in Hove and electoral role entries in Lancing, a photo from a prep school in Worthing, and some letters, today browned like urn-stewed tea, from an address in Southsea, are testament to a noticeable marine drift.

The full wash-up, as it were, would have to wait until the 1930s and in family lore was latterly explained by oblique and euphemistic allusions to the Wall Street crash and a loss of money. This came, I think, not out of self-aggrandisement but a more genuine incomprehension at a turn of events that saw my grandfather move from stockbroking in London to labouring in a chalk pit in Shoreham. And since he was paid by the hour, having all of his teeth extracted during one lunch break and returning to an afternoon of shovelling with sore and bloody gums while a false set were made. From hereafter though, the clan would largely be engaged with varying degrees of success (and sanity), in such time-honoured seaside professions as novelty trinket vendors, guesthouse proprietors, restauranteurs, publicans, cafe owners and windsurfing instructors.

In the whole scheme of English seaside-ing, our contributions to the field would be modest to say the least. When it comes down to it, our legacy consists, firstly, of a quite novel for its day, pirate-themed eatery in Polperro in Cornwall. Called The Jolly Roger, its walls were lined with real cutlasses and its battered cod and chips were commended by Franklin Engelmann on BBC Radio's *Down Your Way*. I vividly recall that its leatherette-bound menus were decorated with compass points and written in an indecipherable copperplate script that made ordering food feel like a hunt for buried treasure. The cutlasses, as I learned much later, had been picked up at job lot in some auction in the 1950s by the ever-canny Great-uncle Bob. They were of questionable vintage but against a backdrop of spongy-white plaster and dark wood beams, and offset by Toby jugs and brass ships barometers, their buccaneering credentials appeared unimpeachable. To an impressionable child, anyway.

Secondly, there was a range of conch-shell shaded electric lamps. These were unveiled to enormous, if sadly all too brief, acclaim, at the Ideal Home Exhibition at Earls Court in 1964.

And that's it, really. A failure to produce anything of a more lasting significance hasn't, however, ever dented a commitment to coastal topographies that continues to be close to absolute.

It was, then, in a less-than-latent desire to assert my own independence that I upped sticks for college in dry-docked Birmingham at the earliest opportunity. From there I headed down to London, which I instantly fell in love with, and where I have remained ever since. For a long time I nursed such an antipathy to the region of my birth that I avoided visiting it for five years. Even road signs in south London indicating sea-bound routes made me distinctly queasy for a while. In retrospect, I can see this was all tied up with a desire to convince myself, as much as anyone else, that London was my home. Rather like a divorcé with a new partner, denigrating the past was the easiest means of showing fealty to the present. But the salt water in my blood would inevitably draw me back, as a tripper, anyway.

When I first left, though, there seemed scarcely anything worth returning for. Unemployment was high, over 18 per cent in Brighton. Homelessness and smack were everywhere. Hotels abandoned by holidaymakers were doing their best to provide sanctuary for the uncared for in the community. And, in some areas along this coast, what wasn't a charity shop was boarded up. And what wasn't boarded up was burnt out. The pervasive atmosphere was one of hopelessness.

Typing these words some twenty years later, during another recession, things look different, to say the least. Over the past decade my own prejudices about any possible rehabilitation of seaside towns, challenged slowly but steadily by the gravitation of valued friends to the coast and even meeting my wife at a music festival in a decayed holiday camp at Camber Sands, have ebbed away.[4] And like an incoming tide whose encroaching waves seem barely perceptible until they have claimed the entire sands, by the summer of 2009, the summer of the staycation, the English seaside had acquired the imprimatur of cool.

With the pound tanking and the economy going belly-up, holidaying at home was rendered stylishly thrifty and patriotic to boot. Such was its cachet that politicians, previously keen to decamp to Barbadian villas or yachts off Corfu for the summer, now on the rack over expenses, lost no time in espousing their virtues and promising extra investment funds, in studiously casual seafront press shoots. Then in a television interview in the run-up to the 2010 general election, a teary-eyed Gordon Brown confessed that he'd proposed to his wife Sarah on a windswept beach at the start of the Millennium. That beach was, admittedly, in Fife. But the point had been made.

4   Though on trips to some previously unvisited seaside towns for this book and at the mercy of B&Bs with set breakfast times, unsure about entering hostile-looking pubs and ambling along sopping esplanades, listless and with not quite enough to do, my adolescent self was reborn.

Looking back, it was perhaps in those early days of the new century that our rapprochement with the English seaside really began. It was in 2000, after all, that Margate girl-made-good Tracey Emin sold her Whitstable beach hut to Charles Saatchi for £75,000.

That was art. But eight years on, Channel 4 News could only marvel that huts were changing hands at £40,000 a time in Southwold. And at Mudeford Spit in Dorset there was reputedly a waiting list of six years just to rent one. As Matt Carroll, writing about this vogue for seaside shacks in the *Guardian* noted, what was once thought 'run down' was 'now seen as "delightfully kitsch"'.

Television shows such as BBC's *Coast*, whose first episodes were broadcast in 2005 and concluded with Nicholas Crane asking British viewers to remember that they were 'never more than 72 miles from the sea,' sang the seaside's praises once again. A seemingly unconnected new glossy magazine with the same name arrived almost contiguously to present seaside-ing-it as a happening lifestyle option.

Far from being provincial backwaters, beach towns (or so estate agents in Shoreham, St Leonards, Ramsgate and Folkestone kept telling everyone), were at the forefront of cosmopolitan leisure-ing and urban migration. Just as the inner city slums of Notting Hill, Islington, Shoreditch, or Spitalfields had been reclaimed, first by immigrants, exiles and artists and then by investment bankers, so deliquescing resorts, once judged only fit for the elderly and asylum seekers, were pronounced ripe for gentrification.

From Bournemouth to Broadstairs and Blackpool to Southend, soon no resort worth its (sea) salt was without its gastro eateries or luxury boutique hotels. Art Deco wrecks like the Midland in Morecambe and the De La Warr Pavilion in Bexhill were restored. Art festivals came to Folkestone, and contemporary galleries with swish new buildings opened at St Ives (the Tate), Eastbourne (the Towner) and were in the pipeline for Margate (the Turner Contemporary) and Hastings (the Jerwood). Deal and Littlehampton, the latter famed in my youth only for having the highest concentration of venereal disease for a town of its size, or so it was always claimed, were suddenly home to architecturally interesting 'designer' cafes.

On closer inspection, the picture, almost inevitably, was slightly less rosy. A report by the TUC in 2009 found that despite an increase in visitor numbers of two million in the past two years, unemployment in seaside towns had continued to rise, and sharply. Government figures released in January 2010 showed that numbers of those out of work in Weston-Super-Mare had increased by a half in the year. In Margate, 8.5 per cent of its population was claiming unemployment benefit – twice the national rate. Research by the Centre for Cities discovered that the lowest average full-time wage in the UK, at £349 a week, was to be had in Hastings, while the accountants Wilkins Kennedy concluded that in 2008/9 'the average rate of personal insolvencies in coastal towns was almost one third higher than the national average' (at 20.6 per 10,000 adults, compared with 15.7 across the country). On drug-related deaths, too, seaside resorts proved to be in a league of their own. According to data collated by a team at St George's, University of London, Brighton recorded more between 2007 and 2009 than anywhere else in Britain. The second worst place was Blackpool.

But such grim statistics aside, the sudden fashionability of the seaside, a revival of coastal spa breaks and speculation in coastal culture and property among the chattering classes, has marked, in a sense, a return to the very origins of the English seaside as a destination. And in the scheme of this island's lively and lengthy history, it actually hasn't been a destination for all that long. Like football and the railways, the seaside is a distinctly English and largely nineteenth-century invention, one that we subsequently exported to the rest of the world. And similarly had to sit back and watch as the rest of the world, blessed in certain quarters with better weather and sandier sands, has refined the formula and left us rather behind. A situation only exacerbated when cheap flights began allowing us to leave our own shores and sample those faraway beaches for ourselves.

But if we made the seaside, it in turn made us by inculcating notions about health, leisure and the rightful pursuit of pleasure that endure to this day. Its allure may seem elemental and surrounding us, the sea itself has quite obviously influenced every aspect of the nation's life. But the seaside is, nevertheless, deeply cultural. Its history is a part of our national history. Since almost everyone in England has been to the seaside at one time or another, it almost always forms some part of our own personal histories. No other element of the English landscape is experienced quite so universally, arguably. But then like the weather, there is a lot of it and while its range and character varies wildly, it usually boils down to similar combinations of predictably unpredictable dampness.

This book, accordingly, is really an attempt to consider what its story says about us and what stories in turn we've told ourselves about the seaside. To try to see how and why the seaside has become such a powerful part of the narrative of the nation. What is it, for example, about a British beach that is enough to make a great train robber like Ronnie Biggs turn himself in for the chance of a pint by the sea at Margate before he dies?

In conversations with transatlantic friends in particular, it's struck me that in many respects our seaside towns are quite like pubs. We let our hair down, as it were, in both and are prone to claim the medicinal qualities of sea air and drink. Americans, of course, have bars; hostelries that are sometimes literally countertops. Everything in such establishments revolves around providing intoxicants with minimal fuss and maximum efficiency; the customer on their stool is only ever a foot or so of polished wood away from the next snifter. (And funds permitting, the pace of refills can even be sped up by increasing the size of tips.) You drink for the most part facing the optics and the beer taps. Or, perhaps after two or three and when the rest of the room gets too much, looking down at your glass on the countertop. The main focus here is alcohol. Until you can't focus any more, that is.

Vertical drinking zones and what-have-you have altered the character of many an English boozer, (hostelries and persons), in more recent times. But, like American bars,

Wish You Were Here

most pubs adhere to a style of decor and service that is bound up with the semantics of their name. We guzzle our poisons in venues that still quite assiduously doff their caps to the coaching inn or a version of it from a Peek Freans seasonal biscuit tin: all Mr Pickwick, hunting horns, bad pictures, gilt mirrors and horse brasses. Getting a drink can involve a good degree of effort and, like buying at an auction or betting on a horse, requires a passing knowledge of specific customs, phrases, nudges, winks and nods.

The English seaside, surely, is much the same. With a few notable exceptions, Atlantic City and Miami say, American beachfronts, though usually in private ownership and centred around private enclaves, seem as pared down as their bars: clapboard houses, the odd grand building, a surf station but largely some sea, some sand and not much else. The British, on the other hand, appear incapable of approaching the ocean unless a journey to the shore, much as to an alcoholic drink, is accompanied by some suitably diverting architecture and an above average chance of some other entertainments along the way.

Why that might be the case is what I set out to find out. The development of the English seaside has been charted many times and my debt to the hundreds of books published on the subject before is enormous. Although I am to a certain extent a prodigal son returning to my roots, this was never intended to be any kind of personal story. Though I will appear from time to time. Like the few shoreside pebbles and shells among millions that we choose to pick up and carry home, what follows probably owes as much to my curious enthusiasms and the odd geographical bias as any attempt to chart the whole terrain. But then, what more curious a terrain is there in England than the seaside, with its semi-naked bathers and quasi-Oriental piers?

I

Half in Love With Easeful Death

Scarborough was Sick and the Ocean was a Monster
– Send for Dr Brighton – The Maladies of the
Monarchy – The Sublime Satire of Jane Austen –
Oh TB Beside the Sea with Charlotte Brontë

All was not calm in the Sea of Tranquility Guest House. Or perhaps it would be more accurate to say, all was not *well* in the Sea of Tranquility Guest House. For on this particular morning the usual lulling, ambient sounds of seagulls and waves had been cut by the harsher tones of someone closer to hand coughing and then blowing their nose. Like a child in a playgroup alternating between a toy drum and a kazoo, this noise was incessant but the beat far too irregular to blank out entirely. Each fresh snort and hack, while expected, seemed to assault with the same force as the one that had initially woken me, besting my alarm by a full hour. That this din was emanating from several floors below did little to quell its power to disturb. It may perhaps even have added to it. The nearby stairwell, while carpeted, serving to amplify rather than muffle the racket.

Clearly a once imposing property, the Sea of Tranquility is a sturdy Victorian terraced house in the South Cliff part of Scarborough; the main town is pitched between two bays, the North and South Cliffs. Today the South Bay, the more obviously seaside-y of the two has a certain feral quality. Tamed by man over the centuries, it is wilder than the less populated North Bay. But in the era when the Sea of Tranquility was built it was said that 'the best people resided' in the South. Most of its capacious, high-ceilinged rooms, however, long ago succumbed to division. And more recent looking modifications to accommodate en suite shower units, coupled with an exterior wall decoration heavy on pastel shades and a front patio loaded with mock toadstools and elfin folk, did their best to undermine any lingering signs of frock-coated grandiosity. Still, it had charm, as did its landlady Suzette, the source, as I discovered, of the sneezing.

Suzette was a woman in late middle age whose dress and distracted manner could easily lead you to believe she'd wandered out of an early 1970s Gong concert during a protracted flute solo. Her hippy-ish demeanour masked an admirably canny operator. Certainly her excuses for penny-pinching amendments to the breakfast menu were too ingenious not to admire. The substitution of tinned grapefruit for fresh because 'the ones in the shop weren't big enough' particularly impressive. But any remonstration seemed futile when each excuse was accompanied – and they always were – with the sweetest of smiles and a practically rhetorical, 'You don't mind luv, do you now?'

Though her own quarters were in the basement flat, Suzette normally pottered about the ground floor dining room – a Dickensian-esque parlour where every spare surface was littered with porcelain shepherdesses and tinkers or framed sepia photographs of stayed maidens and stiff-backed bewhiskered gents. For Gerry, the only other guest during my stay there in April, a plasterer from Leyton in town for a TUC Black Workers Conference, the presence of a row of knitted Gollies in the fireplace might have been harder to swallow than the tinned grapefruit. But he bore them and the inevitable, 'You don't mind luv, do you now?' with equanimity. Accepting Suzette's added caveat that 'they weren't coloured people when I was young, just dolls' with equal good grace and a brief shrug as he tucked into his bacon, sausage, eggs and a slice.

Suzette didn't eat with us but once the main business of serving was over she'd take a place on an adjacent table to chat. In between folding napkins and good-naturedly besmirching neighbouring hoteliers she would swallow a sequence of multicoloured tablets from an array of plastic pots lined up on the cloth in front of her. This arrangement seemed to provide a bizarre mirror to the sauce bottles and marmalade laid out for breakfast. And in my more fanciful moments I liked to imagine that she was a visitor from the lunch-will-be-a-pill future scientists once promised us. But she'd usually bring me back to earth by making an odd nodding gesture with her head. An allusion, usually extremely cryptic, to some condition I assumed to be menopausal would then follow.

Now, though, she had a cold. A large box of tissues had joined the pills, whose ranks appeared to have expanded to accommodate a range of flu remedies and she was casting germs all around (or something). It was unfortunate, given that I'd picked this guesthouse to avoid catching a bug. Scouting around for somewhere to stay in Scarborough, I had become kind of fixated by the Grand. 'Once the largest hotel in Europe', this crenellated building with four domed towers, part Russian Kremlin, part French chateau, still dominates the skyline of Scarborough's South Bay. Fashioned in yellow brick in the 1860s in a style that is as Oriental as it is Gothic, it looks like a majestic, monstrous, sandcastle. One that has a near but tide-ravaged twin on the opposite corner of the bay with the ancient ruin of a fort. But a friend had warned me off, detailing a depressing catalogue of multiple closures for outbreaks of infectious gastroenteritis. A hotel where you apparently have to wash your hands with liquid soap before entering does not inspire confidence. And so I'd ended up at the Sea of

Tranquility. And given my general propensity to pick up ailments, I knew it wouldn't be long before I was on two packs of Kleenex Pocket Balsam a day. And indeed it wasn't.

But there seemed a kind of poetic justice about this. For English seaside resorts at the outset, and Scarborough, as arguably the first, especially, were primarily for the unwell. The word 'resort' itself, deriving from the Old French *resortir*, retains strands of its earlier meaning that captures this perfectly. It's something you turn to for assistance. The earliest visitors 'turned' to the coast for their health, and it is a testament to their desperation to get well that they did.

Previously, the ocean had been regarded as an aquatic monster-dwelling region either best avoided or treated with superstition and fear by the sailors and fishermen whose work brought them into unavoidable contact with it. It was a realm from which boat-borne rapers and pillagers and land-grabbing foreign invaders frequently emerged.

As an event that changed the course of English history, along with forever linking the painful death of the nation's last Anglo-Saxon king with a seaside town, the Battle of Hastings – fought, to be pedantic, at nearby Battle, its name one of those commemorative coinages that means it should really be the Battle of Battle – would continue to loom large in the collective psyche until Nelson's day.

Those who lived near the sea and plied its waters were only too aware of the astonishing natural savagery of which it was capable. Daniel Defoe provides a salient reminder of just how dangerous it was to live and work on the coast in the past. In a passage from *A Tour Through the Whole Island of Great Britain* on Brighton or 'Bright Helmston', which he visited in the 1690s when it was 'a poor fishing town, old built', he writes, 'The sea is very unkind to this town and has by continual enchroachments, so gained upon them, that in a little time more they might reasonably expect it would eat up the whole town, above 100 houses having been devoured by the water in a few years past.'

A further indication of the uneasy – in every sense of the word – relationship such towns endured with the ocean can immediately be discerned in their original layouts. As an article on the development of seaside resorts from *The Times* back in August 1860 noted, 'The Old Town is perhaps half a mile inland, and turned as far away from the sea as possible, for the fishermen were by no means desirous of always looking at the sea or having the salt spray blowing in their windows. They got as far back as they could . . . for the sake of shelter and repose.'

Scarborough, as it happens, is a classic example of this type of settlement. One of its oldest surviving streets, The Bolts, is a spindly, crooked rear artery some way from the foreshore. Running horizontally to the quayside, its row of dwellings, lilting, wonky-toothed constructions, face each other. The main views are of the opposing houses. A rear wall alone, itself shielded by other defences closer to the water, would have met the sea when they were first built. And no doubt pretty reluctantly.

Time has drained the whole notion of deliberately choosing to be beside the sea of its radicalism. But it reflects a quite astonishing transformation in attitudes to coastal, and indeed the whole, landscape in Britain between the eighteenth and early nineteenth century. We have to imagine the almost unthinkable: an England without sea views.

An island race, completely indifferent, if not downright averse, to the stuff that defined and surrounded them.

Before the eighteenth century the sea was essentially prized for the most part as a kind of vast moat, protecting fortress Britain's green and pleasant lands. As Margaret Drabble notes in her study of the nation's landscape and literature *A Writer's Britain*, 'Appreciation of the grandeurs and beauties of the sea was largely a Romantic innovation.' Just as troubadour minstrels are said to have propagated the whole notion of romance and love in pre-Renaissance France, so it was writers and poets on the eve of the industrial revolution who were to alter our perceptions of the oceans.

One of the earliest proponents in this country of the opinion that the sea could be experienced 'romantically' was Joseph Addison. What made Addison such a radical was his belief that beauty could lie in landscapes and objects that much more tidy-minded Classicists had previously regarded as irregular, disorderly, if not plain ugly.

In an essay for the *Spectator* in 1712, he wrote, 'there is none which affects my imagination so much as the sea or ocean. I cannot see the heaving of this prodigious bulk of waters, even in a calm, without a very pleasing astonishment; but when it is worked up in a tempest, so that the Horizon on every side is nothing but foaming billows and floating mountains, it is impossible to describe the agreeable horrour that rises from such a prospect. A troubled ocean, to a man who sails upon it, is, I think, the biggest object that he can see in motion, and consequently give his imagination one of the highest kinds of pleasure that can arise from greatness.'

This concept of a sort of 'agreeable horrour' would also prove central to the principles subsequently set down by Edmund Burke in 1757 in his influential tract *On the Sublime and the Beautiful* – virtually the Little Red Book of English Romanticism. Here Burke argued that the ocean, was 'an object of no small terror'. And terror either more openly or latently was 'the ruling principle of the sublime'.

So in a way, the seaside can quite feasibly be said to move from the sublime to the ridiculous.

Though wildly overstated and often contradicted, one of the characteristics of English culture has been a marked disdain for intellectuals and highfalutin ideas. We like to see ourselves as stoutly pragmatic, with even our most radical thinkers appealing to 'common sense' rather than abstract rationalism when advancing their theories. The Dublin-born Burke is as good an example of this as any, his own stress on history, tradition and the institutions of the state means he is hailed as the father of modern Conservatism.

But it is a testament of sorts to the currency of his aesthetics and their sudden application to the coasts, that Jane Austen, with her resolutely English dislike of pretension and intense emotion (and *sense* would always triumph over sensibility in Austen), should mock them so witheringly in her last, unfinished novel *Sanditon*. Though barely more than a handful of opening chapters, what we have of the book provides an extraordinarily acute, and mercilessly funny, snapshot of the then still emerging mania for the seaside in England. As such it is worth considering in some detail.

Like *Northanger Abbey*, Austen's better-known, and also posthumously published, parody of Gothic fiction, *Sanditon* has little truck with the evolving tenets of Romanticism. In one scene, the book's heroine Charlotte Heywood, 'a very pleasing young woman of two and twenty', is treated to a lecture in newfangled oceanic wonderment by Sir Edward Denham, one of the eponymous resort's bigwigs.

'He began', Austen states, 'in a tone of great Taste & Feeling, to talk of the Sea & the Sea shore – & ran with Energy through all the usual Phrases employed in praise of their Sublimity, & descriptive of the undescribable Emotions they excite in the Mind of Sensibility – The terrific Grandeur of the Ocean in a Storm, its glassy surface in a calm, its Gulls & its Samphire, & the deep fathoms of its Abysses, its quick vicissitudes, its direful Deceptions, its Mariners tempting it in Sunshine & overwhelmed by the sudden Tempest – All were eagerly & fluently touched; – rather commonplace perhaps – but doing very well from the Lips of a handsome Sir Edward, – and she could not but think him a Man of Feeling – till he began to stagger her by the number of his Quotations, & the bewilderment of some of his sentences.'

Written when Austen herself was battling against fatal illness, *Sanditon* is all the more affecting for the scepticism with which it also views then widely promoted claims about the benefits to health of sea air and water.

The book opens with a minor post chaise accident and the hunt for a surgeon. A sequence of events that Austen uses to introduce us to Sophie and her family, the sensible Heywood clan, and the Parkers, coastal landowners engaged in redeveloping their estates at Sanditon.

Having sprained his ankle tumbling out of the coach, it emerges that Mr Parker has been roaming the nearby countryside trying to nab a medical man to help promote his town as an up-and-coming health resort. He himself is a fervent advocate of marine cures, arguing that even a little of Sanditon's 'Bracing Sea Air' will be more than enough to get him back on his twisted limb again. Austen has Parker holding the opinion that, '[No] person could be really well, no person (however upheld for the present by fortuitous aids of exercise and spirits in a semblance of health) could be really in a state of secure and permanent health without spending at least six weeks by the sea every year. The sea air and sea bathing together were nearly infallible, one or the other of them being a match for every disorder of the stomach, the lungs or the blood. They were anti-spasmodic, anti-pulmonary, anti-septic, anti-bilious and anti-rheumatic. Nobody could catch cold by the sea; nobody wanted appetite by the sea; nobody wanted spirits; nobody wanted strength. Sea air was healing, softening, relaxing – fortifying and bracing – seemingly just as was wanted – sometimes one, sometimes the other. If the sea breeze failed, the sea bath was the certain corrective; and where bathing disagreed, the sea air alone was evidently designed by nature for the cure.'

Like the best satires, the force of the comedy comes from its basis in reality. Austen, an unhappy resident of the spa town Bath, had spent pleasant times in Lyme (Regis) and Teignmouth and also visited Ramsgate and Worthing and so was more than acquainted with the coastal milieu she describes. Savages, really. She'd witnessed first hand the rise of seaside resorts, in large part through aristocratic patronage.

It is interesting to consider what future, if any, English coastal towns might have gone on to enjoy had the genetic disorders of our royals not been so pronounced. In the Georgian period the reigning Hanoverian house was arguably one of the sickest in Europe. Consequently its members were perhaps more willing than most to submit themselves to whatever faddish remedies their surgeons suggested, no matter how gruesome on occasions. And by the eighteenth century, royal physicians were advising their masters to both drink, and bathe in, seawater.

These treatments, though based on ancient folk remedies, were really developed as modish adjuncts to the type of spa mineral water cures that had been knocking around these islands since Roman times. Following the conversion to Christianity, such spas had been sanctioned as 'holy wells'. Dedicated to saints, they were sites of religious pilgrimage and visited, much like Lourdes today, by the poor, the sick, the devoted and the merely deluded. From the medieval period onwards, the sulphur waters at Bath had been highly acclaimed for their medicinal qualities – their efficacy vouchsafed over the following centuries by a client base, if you'll forgive the modern jargon, that would include monarchs, their consorts, mistresses and some of the realm's most distinguished peers, courtiers and hangers-on. By the 1700s and with Richard 'Beau' Nash as its dandy in residence and master of ceremonies, Bath had consolidated its position as Britain's pre-eminent and exclusive watering place, while spas at Buxton, Knaresborough, Harrogate, Cheltenham, Tunbridge Wells, which was only thirty-six miles from the capital, and later those on London's outer suburban rim at Epsom, Richmond, Islington and Hampstead, would all vie for attention. Meccas for the affluent ill and destinations prized for their social as much as their clinical facilities, they were the direct precursors to seaside resorts – and the first seaside resorts, with their assembly rooms, theatres, libraries, reading rooms, as well as their crescents and terraces, parades and promenades, were near replicas of the inland spas.

In *Sanditon*, one of Austen's prime targets is the worried-well or the worried well-off: the kind of financially secure malingerers who appeared to be suffering from little more than 'the malaise of what to do and where to do it'. And at this point in history, were choosing to do it by the sea rather than at an inland spa.

It is Mr Parker's sisters Diana and Susan who endure the brunt of Austen's scorn for all but abandoning themselves to the pleasures of ill health on the coast. This sickly, thin pair are reported to pass their days indoors imbibing patent remedies, having teeth pulled and generally encouraging their youngest brother, the corpulent Arthur to loll about by a midsummer fire eating buttered toast.

As a portrait of hypochondria it is among Austen's finest comic efforts. However, the degree to which disease and death stalked the land in the author's time can't be stressed enough. The kind of health we now take for granted was virtually impossible before the arrival of antibiotics – or even what Edmund Gosse, writing shortly before that in 1907, called 'the invention of sanitary science'. Skin disorders, blood poisoning and a plethora of other bacterial infections bundled up under such catch-all terms as 'colic', 'malaise' and 'weakness' were widespread and potentially fatal.

Austen herself would die at forty-one from either TB or Addison's disease, but by then had already lost at least one potential suitor and seen four of her sisters-in-law die from complications after childbirths. Her fictions, not unsurprisingly, are stuffed with genteel invalids, and illness is a recurring preoccupation of her characters, from the draught-dodging and gruel-eating Mr Woodhouse in *Emma* to the forever 'sensitive' Mary Musgrove in *Persuasion*.

It is also worth remembering that all of Austen's finished novels were published during the Regency period. *Sense and Sensibility*, the first to make it into print, appeared in 1811, the year that the Prince of Wales was granted stewardship of the throne, his father, George III having been declared insane. We'll return to George later. But sickness was simply ubiquitous and when it came to infirmities, the upper classes in this period were peculiarly advantaged. They alone possessed the time, the money and the inbreeding to incubate a range of afflictions that the poor couldn't afford. (Or certainly didn't live long enough to enjoy, anyway.)

'Gout', the eighteenth century wit, the Reverend Sydney Smith, once quipped, 'loves ancestors and genealogy, it needs five or six generations of gentlemen or nobleman to give it full vigour.' And as a condition brought on by an abnormally high concentration of uric acid in the blood, and exacerbated by the consumption of heavy, rich food and alcohol, it was virtually endemic among the English aristocracy. Though in an era when precise medical diagnosis was in its infancy and folklore decreed it 'a disease of the better sort', its name did tend to be bandied around somewhat indiscriminately. How to treat it was equally hit and miss.

As Roy Porter argues in his history of medicine, *Blood and Guts*, before the twentieth century, 'the pharmacopoeia resembled a box of blanks'. For two millennia everyone muddled along with a mix of two basic therapeutic options: the Hippocratic and the Heroic. Under the Hippocratic, physicians could call upon such time-honoured techniques as watching and waiting, bed rest, tonics, soothing words and hope. With the Heroic, meanwhile, the doctor had bloodletting, violent purges and what Porter refers to as, 'some pet nostrum of his own' to unleash upon their patients.

Ocean brine was just one such 'pet nostrum' deployed.

One of its earliest recorded advocates was Dr Robert Wittie, a pamphleteering medical practitioner from York. Little information about Wittie himself survives; but from his writings we know he was a hydropathic evangelist and early campaigner for temperance, famed for putting forward the theory that the Romans had enjoyed longer lives because they consumed more water and women were forbidden wine. In 1667 or thereabouts he published *Scarborough Spaw*, a quackish but evidently quite successful hagiography championing the medicinal powers of a mineral water spa at Scarborough, then a small fishing port. This spa, he maintained, had been discovered in around 1627 by Mrs Farrow 'a gentlewoman of good repute' and since had become 'the usual physic of the inhabitants of Scarborough' and by reputation was, apparently, 'well known to the citizens of York, and the gentry of the country.'

It was this spa that in the wake of Wittie's proselytising initially became the engine of Scarborough's subsequent prosperity. When 'an earthquake' in 1737 destroyed the original 'Spaw House' and 'the waters were for a time lost', the borough authorities led 'a diligent' – for which read desperate – and ultimately successful search to recover them. Such were their value to the local economy by then.[5] Though these waters have not been drunk since the 1960s when the well was sealed off, their name lives on in a 'Complex' – a conference centre cum venue with a theatre, cafe, terraces and shops on the South bay.

But along with the spa, Wittie also argued that the local seawater, if imbibed and bathed in, was a capital cure for gout, killed off all manner of worms and was efficacious for 'drying up superfluous humours' – the four sustaining bodily juices whose imbalance were held responsible for most diseases.

Wittie's opinions about seawater were reiterated some thirty years later by another medical man, Sir John Floyer. Floyer was the author of *An Enquiry into the Right Uses and Abuses of Hot, Cold Temperate Baths in England* (1697) and a *History of Cold Water Bathing* (1702) and in the latter book maintained that, 'since we lived on an Island, and have the Sea about us, we cannot want an excellent Cold Bath, which will preserve our Healths, and cure many diseases, as our Fountains [spas] do.' In his opinion, bathing in – and drinking – seawater was invaluable for treating ulcers, scabs, leprosy, corns, tumours, pains of the limbs, gonorrhoea, arthritis and gout.

---

5 By 1777, the spa was considered fashionable enough to provide the setting for Sheridan's bowdlerised version of Vanbrugh's comedy, *The Relapse*, which he retitled, *A Trip to Scarborough*. As a portrait of the seaside in these times it is, however, worse than useless. Even one of its earliest critics complained that, since Sheridan had moved the action to a watering place he might have expected 'some display of the manners and customs of an English spaw; but no such delineation is attempted.'

By at least 1732, when the Duchess of Marlborough, a scurvy-afflicted veteran of spas at Tunbridge Wells and Bath, arrived in Scarborough, sea bathing was on the way to becoming an established quasi-medical procedure, at least in this one northern health retreat. Although Marlborough appears to have confined herself to purging on the local mineral waters, in letters to her daughter she described seeing the Duchess of Manchester venturing into the sea each morning as part of her therapeutic regimen. In a near-contemporary engraving of the seafront by John Setterington, the shore is dotted with wheeled wooden chariots, stilted Romany wagons that are clearly primitive bathing machines.

And if a missive from Lord Chesterfield in 1733 is to be believed, bathing was widespread enough for the government to consider taxing it. Again writing from Scarborough, Chesterfield reported that the people of the town were in a 'great consternation' over rumours from London about a levy they feared would 'ruin them.' (Though tellingly, this was the same year that Robert Walpole's government was rocked by an excise crisis over tobacco and wine, so such rumours were probably rife.)

'As bathing in the sea is becoming the general practice of both sexes', Chesterfield wrote, 'and as the Kings of England have always been allowed to be masters of the sea, every person so bathing shall be gauged and, pay so much per foot as their cubical bulk amounts to.' Chesterfield himself didn't give much credence to the plan, which in the end vanished without troubling the statute books.

However generally sea bathing may have been practised, it wasn't until the 1750s, when another medic entered the fray, that the seaside finally became truly voguish. Dr Richard Russell, a London physician with a fashionable practice in Lewes in Sussex, had observed that the local people 'made use of sea-water' to treat ailments. Dosing his own wealthy patients with it for a fee, he was impressed enough with the results (or the easy money to be had) to move his practice to Brighthelmstone, then a dank, smelly fishing village and penned *A Dissertation on the use of Seawater in the Diseases of the Glands particularly The Scurvy, Jaundice, King's Evil, Leprosy, and the Glandular Consumption*. Published at first in Latin in 1750, and then in English two years later, this tract, along with the doctor's presence in a seaside town that was barely fifty miles from the capital, really sealed the future of the seaside resort in this country.

The effect on Russell's adopted home was dramatic to say the least. What in 1759, the year of the doctor's death, was still a humble backwater of six unpaved streets and flint and mortar houses, had by the Act of Union become a thriving, cosmopolitan resort with fine new buildings. The ugly duckling Brighelmstone had by then been reborn, rebranded if you must, as the swan 'Brighton'.

Like Wittie and Floyer before him, Russell regarded sea-water as a panacea. In his view it had been designed by the 'omniscient Creator of All Things' as a 'Kind of common Defence against the Corruption and Putrification of Bodies'. It was particularly useful against 'the Consumption', which he noted, 'greatly afflicts our Island', but could also work wonders on 'the Disorders of the internal glands', and was no slouch either against cirrhosis, leprosy, scrofula, scurvy or dropsy.

Russell's cures involved bathing in the sea and drinking its water. If the latter sounds unpleasant, the brine was often combined with a variety of repulsive preparations, ranging from crab's eyes to burn sponges and tar, that wouldn't be out of place in *Macbeth*. Inevitably, these tonics were supplemented by regular bloodlettings. None of this would have seemed especially strange in Russell's time and, far beyond it, sea bathing remained a highly medicalised activity. (In 1811, one guide to Scarborough was still advising would-be bathers 'to consult some gentleman in the medical line' before even thinking of heading into the sea.)

To enhance the effects of the water on the constitution, bathers were usually instructed to dip before breakfast. Towels soaked in seawater and then dried were often used to ensure that the skin retained as much health-giving saline as possible. Wearing any kind of costume was considered effeminate and thought likely to inhibit the flow of sea-water to the body, so men and boys went naked.

Women and girls usually wore long flannel quasi-baptismal gowns that, combined with the cart-like machines that carried them into the ocean, helped to protect their modesty. Though naked bathing was not unheard of among women in the earliest years. Initially, both sexes appear to have bathed in the same part of the sea. As numbers grew, however, segregated areas, or time slots in some resorts, Blackpool (celebrated in 1788 as 'an abode of health and scene of amusement') for instance, evolved.

Upper-class bathers rarely ventured into the sea alone. They were attended to by 'dippers'. Cast, at least by those who chose to record their deeds, as larger than life characters in the Shakespearean comic servant vein, their task was to immerse their charges in the water. (Strong arms, a background in midwifery or the navy and an inventive way with a limited vocabulary, seemingly, were among the main qualifications for the job.) At this stage, no one went into the sea to swim as such. Those that were actually able to swim were in the minority in any case, which was another reason to have a 'dipper' on hand. The main object of entering the sea was not to engage in pelagic athletics but to soak up the restorative brine.

Some six years after Russell's death, the Duke of Gloucester, George III's youngest brother, became the first of the Hanoverian royals to visit Brighton. The Duke was no stranger to ill health or unorthodox elixirs. Falling ill in Trent while on a tour of Italy in 1771, he became so emaciated that his doctors ordered him to suck at 'the breasts of some healthy country women that were sent for from the mountains'. He recovered and lived for another three decades. His example at Brighton was soon followed by the Dukes of Marlborough, York and Cumberland who all took houses in the town. Cumberland, who was also a patron of Margate, where the Royal Sea Bathing Infirmary was established in 1796, rented out Dr Russell's former abode on the Steine – a strip of rocky ground up from the foreshore to which for generations fishermen had repaired to dry nets and whittle wood.

When George, the Prince of Wales, paid his first trip to Brighton in September 1783, it was to visit his uncle. However, he ostensibly returned the following July on the advice of his doctors, who believed that sea bathing might ease the swollen glands on his neck.

His father, the King, meanwhile, went to Weymouth in Dorset in 1789 to recover from a 'bilious attack' (possibly the onset of the genetic disorder porphyria) that all too ominously had left him lame and mentally distracted. The town, promoted as a seaside spa by Ralph Allen, a native of Bath, had already come to the attention of the Duke of Gloucester, who built a substantial mansion on the front. This property was to house the King, his Queen, their three daughters and their entourage when they made the first of what proved to be many visits to the town. The novelist Fanny Burney who was a member of the Royal household, was amused by the excessive displays of deference in Weymouth. She noted that every street was 'dressed out . . . with labels of "God save the King": all the shops have it over the doors; all the children wear it in their caps, all the labourers in their hats, and all the sailors in their voices, for they never approach the house without shouting it aloud, nor see the King, or his shadow, without beginning to huzza, and going on to three cheers.'

According to Burney, when the King first went into the sea, his bathing machine was followed by another loaded with fiddlers who struck up the national anthem the moment his head emerged from the water. Ludicrous as this no doubt was, the King's sojourn put the place on the map. Sidmouth would feel similarly blessed after the monarch swung by in 1791. Soon the appearance of even quite minor royals was enough to excite interest in formerly quite undistinguished coastal villages.

In 1798 the King's youngest daughter, Princess Amelia, pitched up at Worthing, a hamlet consisting at that point, in the historian J.A.R. Pimlott's pithy summation, 'of a few miserable cottages'.

Amelia suffered from what in the argot of the era were called 'very delicate nerves' and spent much of her brief life as an invalid. Aged fifteen she'd been diagnosed, bafflingly, with 'tuberculosis of the knee' (consumption, possibly exacerbated by incipient porphyria) and was sent to Worthing for the summer to convalesce. The Prince of Wales, riding over from Brighton, visited her almost daily while she was there, which was another feather in the cap for the town. In subsequent years, however, and with her health worsening, the young Princess was dispatched to the more established Weymouth, where she was subjected to some quite appalling remedies, ultimately to little avail. She was bled, blistered and purged. Her skin was coated with leeches and pierced with quills before she was immersed in hot seawater baths. Prescribed a diet of beef tea, calomel and Madeira wine, she was further medicated with a slew of powders, medicines, restoratives and stimulants, including laudanum. Increasingly sensitive to light, her doctors fitted her bathing machine with a green curtain to shade the glare from the sea on early morning dunks. Despite, or perhaps because of all this, she went into steep decline and died in 1810 aged 27.

However pitiful the royal physicians' track record, their subsequent decision to pack Princess Charlotte off to Southend and Worthing only improved the prospects of both. Although the royals may now have been largely usurped as trendsetters, the lingering (if to my mind, depressing), reverence for the royal family reflects the degree to which their actions once led English habits and customs.

From this distance, the thought of going somewhere where most of the people are ill hardly seems that inviting. There may well be people today fighting to get into The Priory because they like the idea of hanging out with Amy and chums. But, surely, as that old joke about the invalid refusing to go to hospital because it's full of sick people sums up, the most natural thing is to steer clear of the poorly.

Obviously, no one went to Southend or Worthing to get ill. They went there to be, or to get, better. Health was the impetus, even if hypochondria, à la Austen's Parker clan, can't be rejected entirely. And yet in the seaside towns in their infancy there is this odd combination of the ailing and the *beau monde*, a combination they inherited from the spas. If this offers up any deep-seated truths about the British character, it would seem to indicate that we've been a nation of malingerers for centuries. A land, not of hope and glory and stiff upper lips but of easeful death-loving snobbish neurotics, happiest with a soggy handkerchief within easy reach. What it also seems to reflect is a well-rooted strand of Puritanism that demanded a kind of penance – or at least a decent excuse – for idleness or pleasure. But penance done, idleness and pleasure were there to be had for the lucky few.

The nation may have lost America. And the King his marbles. But victories against the French and a growing sense of the country's status as a maritime Imperial power, coupled with the first stirrings of industrialisation and its direct aesthetic corollary, Romanticism, were all at this juncture conspiring to imbue the notion of simply being beside the sea with a unique prestige. One that coastal landowners, property speculators and quack doctors were quick to capitalise upon.

The speed and manner in which this came to pass is again caught quite brilliantly in Austen's *Sanditon*. Though she allows her heroine Charlotte to be roused (if only slightly) by the view of the glistening sea from her bedroom window, Austen is far too much of an Augustan to tolerate Wordsworthian revelries on her watch.[6] Equally, it is patently obvious that we are encouraged to view as absurd the Parkers' abandonment of a perfectly good ancestral pile two miles inland for a new build on the cliffs. In a completed version of the novel, it is easy to imagine the sensible minded Charlotte, having bagged Sidney, the one sane Parker, restoring the natural order of things by setting up home there instead.

The novel is perhaps most bemused, though, by the basic ambition, the desire, to turn a one-time fishing village into a place of fashionable resort. An ambition that Austen judges a rather vulgar, *nouveau riche* pretension, obviously. But one which several entrepreneurs, among them Sir Richard Hotham with his failed, if pioneering, scheme at Hothampton (later Bognor Regis) in the 1790s, were, with varying degrees of success, genuinely trying to pull off in this era.

The arrival of 'Blue Shoes and Nankin Boots' in William Heeley's shoemaking shop in Sanditon, considered an

---

6 Bryon would however mock the poet as a landlubber in *Don Juan*. Of the elder man's obsession with the landscape of his birth he wrote, 'There is a narrowness in such a notion which makes me wish you'd change your lakes for the ocean.'

omen of the town's increasing sophistication by Mr Parker, is used by Austen to illustrate the provincialism of its aspirations. Forever the ticket, never the face, Parker is ridiculed as a prototype of the desperate-to-be-with-it trendy. He is a man who regrets naming his latest abode Trafalgar House now that Waterloo is all the rage. A fault he plans to rectify by building a Waterloo Crescent, the following year.

Yet, as Margaret Drabble has rightly observed, 'the age was on the side of Mr Parker' and, it could be added, Sir Edward Denham. For while elegant Regency buildings rose along the shores of Dorset, Sussex, Kent, Norfolk, Yorkshire and Lancashire, to the consternation of the likes of Charles Lamb who argued that such 'land luggage' was spoiling the natural landscape, the urge to swoon before the oceans only grew. Samuel Taylor Coleridge, voyages to Malta and rhymes to ancient mariners in the past, was to be spotted in the last years of his life assuaging the pangs of his opium addiction with sea breezes at Littlehampton under the watchful eye of his Highgate doctor/landlords, the Gillmans.

And for his (and to a degree Austen's) literary heirs, the seaside would continue to exert a powerful fascination. In a letter to her friend Ellen Nussey shortly before a first trip to the coast in the summer of 1839, Charlotte Brontë wrote, 'The idea of seeing the sea – of being near it – watching its changes by sunrise, sunset, moonlight and noonday – in calm, perhaps in storm – fills and satisfies my mind. I shall be discontented at nothing.' As Ellen would later recall, when Charlotte finally encountered the sea at Bridlington she 'was quite overpowered, she could not speak till she had shed some tears . . . her eyes were red and swollen, she was still trembling . . . for the remainder of the day she was very quiet, subdued, and exhausted.'

Gravely ill with tuberculosis a decade later, her sister Anne would demand to be taken to Scarborough. 'Anne is extremely weak,' Charlotte reported to Nussey on 16 May 1849. 'She herself has a fixed impression that the sea-air will give her chance of regaining strength – that chance therefore she must have.' The trip was, of course, futile. But if Mrs Gaskell's version of events is to be believed, she did at least spend part of her remaining time on earth enjoying one of 'the most glorious sunsets ever witnessed'. And yearned only, and demurely, in those final days to be carried from her easy chair to a place of public worship. Finally departing this life in a house on a site afterwards occupied by The Grand Hotel, her last words to her sister, reputedly, were, 'Take courage, Charlotte. Take courage.'

Advice that, a mere century earlier, was only too commonly given to anyone even approaching the sea.

2

Sex on the Beach

*No Sex Please We're British – Newly-Weds on Hideous
Beds – Conquest at Brighthelmstone – By George IV,
He's Getting It Every Night – French Kissing in the UK*

In the summer months of 1937 and 1938, teams of investigators employed by the Mass Observation Organisation in Bolton headed over to Blackpool to take a look at their mill town subjects relaxing beside the sea. These investigators were obviously serious-minded types, imbued with a sense of the dignity of ordinary lives, a belief in the moral worth of the project's credo to create 'an anthropology of ourselves' and a faith in impartial, empirical, scientifically gathered evidence. Naturally they went to Blackpool expecting 'to see copulation everywhere.'

Having already delighted in the sights and sounds of post-pub, back alley knee-tremblers in Bolton – the ping of braces and the scrape of heels on Lancashire cobbles as undergarments and trousers were lowered and congress commenced, a defiant drunken tussle against a wall with the forces of gravity and inebriation, and the fear of unwanted pregnancy and social approbation all quickening the pulse – this probably wasn't that unreasonable an expectation. And as the MO's subsequent report maintained, wherever their subjects ranged in Blackpool they were certainly assailed by some 'new appeal' to their 'sex instincts'. Or, at least, an 'appreciation of dirty jokes'. No brochure here was without its shots of bathing beauties, those amply proportioned girls happiest in beachwear and when leapfrogging over one another, stroking donkeys' heads or playing with balls on the sands. No gift shop worth its salt was without its saucy Donald McGill postcards, with their images of heaving bosoms, quivering buttocks, wobbly bellies and priapic sticks of rock. Nor amusement arcade without its penny in the slot, crank-the-handle What the Butler Saw peepshow machine – a device that confirmed that life below stairs, for all its indignities, was the still best place to catch posh totty in elaborate states of *déshabillé* and possibly even with a friend or two but invariably in easily removable, if antiquated, stays and smalls.

And as they also noted, 'for a bob', an eyeful of real live girls in skimpies could be had at the Blackpool Funhouse in 1937, where a regular catwalk show was staged that involved a confection of air-jets and voluminous skirts that would scarcely be bettered until Marilyn Monroe strayed over a subway grate at Lexington and 52nd. While the services of a mother and daughter team, who plied that most ancient of trades in a particular hotel between the hours of 8 and 10 p.m., were up for grabs at a mere ten shillings a time – five if business was slack or the older woman was in her cups.

Sex, of one kind or another, was seemingly omnipresent. The Mass Observation wonks were, however, to be severely disappointed by the lack of on the spot licentiousness at the resort. Rather like adolescent schoolboys attempting to mask their virginity by constantly banging on about sex in overcompensation, Blackpool appeared to them to be all talk and no trousers around the ankles. Public 'petting and feeling' was plentiful enough. And for 'older men of scoptophilic tendencies', there were bags of jollies to be had. 'The sands at night' were reported to be 'a happy hunting ground' for such like-to-look types, with any couple lying down in the darker shadows by the piers 'very quickly' acquiring 'a ring of silent, staring individuals around them' and apparently 'without rebuke'. But the observers were forced to conclude that Blackpool did not offer their mill town workers any 'special outlet for sex' and that 'merriment and noise, not sex' were chiefly what was sought.

As ever in England, what was largely at stake here was class. The MO's main prey couldn't afford the fifteen shillings a night needed to secure lodgings 'large enough to enable bedroom manoeuvres free of landlady censorship' as they delicately put it. Where the more affluent might have the run of the sofas in the hotel lounge bar for smooching and a porter who could be summoned to gain entry at any hour, the bolted door and the prospect of a night on a bench greeted the less well-heeled lover should they choose to spoon beyond twelve p.m. And given the necessity to spoon outside, and away from the crowds, this curfew put a severe crimper on the time available 'to go through the inevitable preliminaries which "any decent girl" expected' as one observer was told.

Even accepting that this was the 1930s, when *Lady Chatterley's Lover* remained banned and the Beatles were little more than twinkles in their respective parents' eyes, this rather depressing state of affairs nevertheless appears to undermine a central, arguably essential, tenet of the English seaside's appeal – it's supposed raciness. A raciness, that as those initial, if dashed, expectations of the Mass Observation investigators affirmed, was so deeply seated that its contradiction was almost unconscionable. Sex in English life was hard enough, as those Bolton back alley gymnastics had shown. But to go to the seaside, nearly the only place in England devoted to pleasure, and not try to get a shag would almost be perverse, if not mildly unpatriotic. And yet what could be more British than not having sex? Possibly, not having sex somewhere where it is assumed that everyone else is going at it like rabbits and you are constantly bombarded by images of leapfrogging bathing beauties etc., etc.

And yet, again and again in the popular imagination the seaside is the zone where clothes and sexual inhibitions are shed. In plays and films such as Stanley Houghton's *Hindle Wakes*, the daughters of honest labouring men are supposedly 'ruined' in Blackpool. Or more precisely in this instance in Llandudno, since Houghton's working-class virgin only agrees to do the nasty with the mill owner's son after he promises to take her over the border to a posh Welsh hotel. Tellingly, his inability to sign the register correctly or remember what Mrs Mill Owner's Son normally has for breakfast, are matters of studious indifference to the desk clerk. He's seen it all before, obviously. And how could he not? Seaside hotels, in fiction as in real life, are forever ports where ships meeting in the night can dock.

In the novel *Hangover Square*, Patrick Hamilton's sodden protagonist, the poor besotted George Harvey Bone, convinces himself that once he gets the heartless Netta down to Brighton and the Little Castle hotel she'll finally submit to his charms. She arrives late, drunk and with other men, Peter and George, in tow. Bone is eventually subjected to the sounds of Netta giggling and whispering with Peter as she shares a nightcap of whisky in tooth mugs – and very probably much else besides – in the room next door. His seducer's logic, though, was hardly faulty. For T.S. Eliot's Mr Eugenides in *The Waste Land*, a poem partly composed in Margate, a 'demotic French' invitation to luncheon at London's Cannon Street Hotel is promptly followed by a (presumably dirty) weekend at

Brighton's Metropole. And in common with many, Eliot's own marriage to Vivienne Haigh-Wood was consummated on the coast and in Eastbourne as it happens. Eliot was almost certainly a virgin until then and the wedding night was, bay all accounts, an unmitigated disaster. The Eliots, by default, therefore falling into the category of 'newly-weds making fools of themselves on the hideous beds of seaside lodging houses' that Orwell was later to identify as a recurring feature of Donald McGill's smutty postcards.

That the seaside resort should have become such a realm of erotic possibilities (or embarrassments, and for the English, sex is nearly always treated as a joke; hence McGill's popularity and his prosecution for obscenity in the 1950s, unbelievably) is arguably not as immediately straightforward as it might appear. As we've discussed, their origins as 'arenas of the unwell', as Marwood of *Withnail and I* might have put it, scarcely seems much of a come on, when you think about it. Unless nurses are your bag, which for some people they obviously are and the corollary between sex and death is a longstanding one. But, as many of the invalids at the resorts were there to rid themselves of what William Cobbett dubbed the 'bodily consequences of their manifold sins and iniquities', it could be argued that a curious kind of dissoluteness clung to seaside spas right from the start. As it is, the nautical trade has always been served by what more euphemistically could be termed an 'interdependent hospitality industry', an aspect of maritime life that tended to lend a louche quality to any place where boats were moored. In Nelson's day, the word 'frigate' was, for example, typically used to refer to both type of a ship and a harlot who could be 'boarded' at port. It is, however, only with the arrival of a particular breed of aristocrat, one all but devoted to Sybaritism, that the seaside, in a sense, becomes truly sexy. Though, clearly, the rituals of bathing, however therapeutic were not without their sensual moments.

In his *The Lure of the Sea*, the French cultural historian Alain Corbin persuasively argues that by the dawn of the industrial revolution, the beach was already a highly charged, psychosexual space. Although in his slightly over-excitable reading – think critical theory relayed by the *Fast Show's* Suits You Sir Tailors – every aspect of the seaside becomes a sort of Rorschach inkblot teeming with coded and not so coded messages about our desires. No groyne is ever latent here and a parasol is practically always a stand-in for a hand-job. For women in the eighteenth century, he writes, 'the mere contact of a bare foot on the sand was already a sensual invitation and a barely conscious substitution for masturbation.' In something that was intended as a medical prescription, he argues, such ladies found 'an unexpected freedom that afforded undreamt-of pleasures.' While 'the virile exaltation that a man experienced just before jumping into the water,' he maintains, 'was like that of an erection and quickened by the proximity of women.' Oh la la.

Whether there was genuinely something in the water, as it were (or perhaps merely the possibility of snatching a glimpse of the Continent in the, far far distance) that encouraged onanism to this extent or not, it's easy to see the appeal of frolicking about on the beach for a young buck like George Augustus Frederick, Prince of Wales – a man who would spend much of his first year as Regent incapacitated after twisting his ankle demonstrating the Highland fling. And George was nothing if not a show off.

In a similar feat of lady-impressing daring at Brighton when appalling weather prevented all but the suicidal from bathing, the local dipper Smoker Miles, a leathery old sailor charged with giving those who wanted it a good soaking, had to prevent the Prince from throwing himself into the sea. And while the Regent, once condemned by *The Times* for preferring 'a girl and a bottle to politics and a sermon', did not single-handedly sex up the English seaside, his part in its metamorphosis from a place of repair to a byword for unabashed pleasure can't be underestimated. In Brighton and with the Royal Pavilion, the Prince created a lasting monument to his own excesses. These excesses, although decried in his own day and long afterwards, would nevertheless determine a tone of abandoned enjoyment and spectacle that became a characteristic of English seaside resorts as a whole.

With George too though, the clinical and sexual were initially closely entwined. As has been mentioned earlier, the Prince, like the rest of the Hanoverian line, was plagued by many ailments, including, as a young man, some extremely unsightly swollen glands on his neck. While he sought to disguise them by wearing high collars, a sartorial flourish that duly became rather fashionable, in July 1784 his physicians had prescribed seawater bathing as a possible cure. But in choosing to undertake this palliative in Brighthelmstone, the Prince was seeking the spoonful of sugar as much as the medicine.

Only the previous autumn, George had first visited the town, staying with his uncle and aunt, the Duke and

Duchess of Cumberland. Greeted with a gun salute when he arrived and treated to a ball and a firework display in his honour, the future king had enjoyed a joyous ten days there, further enlivened with trips to the theatre and a stag hunt on the Sussex downs. What the Prince responded to most of all was a mood of ease that prevailed around the Cumberlands. Safely away from his pious and exacting father, King George III, and amidst the far more conducive company of his uncle and aunt's racing set, he caught a whiff of freedom mingling with the sea air.

In a sense the Prince was merely to provide the final Midas touch to Brighton, a royal stroke of luck any scrofulous fishing port would have wished for. But by the time George arrived, the town already boasted two inns that catered for upper-crust visitors: the Castle Tavern and the Old Ship. Each possessed smart assembly rooms, with the Castle's having been designed by John Crunden, a disciple of Robert Adams and the architect of Boodle's Club in St James's, later the model for Ian Fleming's Blades in the James Bond books. But as a pair of sexual adventurers whose numerous affairs and inappropriate marriages were to enrage their elder brother the King, it was arguably the Prince's uncles who had first helped to bequeath a flighty air to the town.

Cumberland, in particular, was regarded with outright dismay by the monarch. Widely thought positively disreputable for running a faro table in his Pall Mall home, he later went on to establish the first horse races at Brighton on White Hawk Down. In 1771, Cumberland had wed Ann Horton (or Houghton), a previously married commoner 'much given to jokes and banter of unparalleled coarseness' and reputedly rather free with her favours too. Their betrothal was widely mocked as the 'conquest at Brighthelmstone' – Cumberland having rented out Dr Russell's former abode on the Steine as his coastal retreat.

The King could scarcely contain his disgust and responded swingeingly. The following year he set about passing the Royal Marriage Act, a piece of legislation that deemed any royal union without the monarch's consent null and void. It subsequently emerged that the Duke of Gloucester had also been secretly married to the Countess Dowager of Waldegrave, the illegitimate granddaughter of Robert Walpole, since 1766. The ensuing family spat only fed young George's appetite for rebellion. And the Prince would contrive a clandestine marriage of his own in 1785 to Mrs Fitzherbert. Fitzherbert was a Roman Catholic and such an alliance, if found legitimate, would have forced him to give up the succession. The union was never publicly acknowledged and later denied as nothing more than an informal exchange of keepsakes. Since the King's approval had not been granted, it would have been judged invalid under the conditions of the act in any case. Brighton would play its part in each of these dubious couplings – and its chief attraction to George, as evidenced by the Cumberlands, was that it was clearly a place to escape or at least avoid censure. Even for the Prince, it represented a holiday from ordinary life. The high collar wearer took to the old girl precisely because wicked ways could be had there. And by George, an inveterate skirt-chaser whose varied romantic career began at sixteen when he seduced one of his mother's maids of honour, they definitely were.

After spending the next two summers in Brighton, the Prince dispatched his cook, Louis Weltje, a former Westphalian gingerbread baker who would eventually die 'at tea' in Hammersmith from a surfeit of his own richly cooked food, to find him a more permanent base in the town. In a somewhat complicated deal that would see the Prince subletting from Weltje to minimise his initial outlay, he acquired the lease on a respectable farmhouse on the Steine. The property had belonged to Tomas Kemp, the MP for nearby Lewes, whose son subsequently became the speculator behind Kemp Town, the residential estate in the eastern part of Brighton laid out by the great Georgian builder Thomas Cubitt – and in the late 1980s a red light district to rival Soho. (As a measure of its relative unimportance back then, Lewes was served by two MPs, while Brighton still had none.)

Ironically, given the money that would eventually be lavished on the Marine Pavilion, thrift was another factor in the Prince's drift to the coast. With severe debts, he planned to save a few quid by closing his main London residence, Carlton House. A not insignificant factor in the nobility's fondness for spas and the seaside was the opportunity to shut up the draughty country pile or stuffy town house, with its attendantly high staffing and heating bills, and rent somewhere smaller and cheaper for a few months of the year. And, importantly, not look like you were penny-pinching. Or at least that any penny-pinching was being undertaken as an ascetic exercise, and for the benefit of your health.

By temperament and inclination, George was not one of life's natural ascetics. Though to begin with he did live more modestly in Brighton than he had in town and was spied contentedly, and even reasonably soberly, pottering about the Steine of an evening. But once taking possession of Kemp's house, described by a contemporary source as 'a singularly pretty, pitturesque cottage in a small piece of ground where a few shrubs and roses shut out the road, and the eye looked undisturbed over the ocean', he promptly commissioned his trusted architectural hand, Henry Holland, to refashion it in a Classical style. The Marine Pavilion that now arose was a creamy Greco-Roman villa whose elegantly restrained style would be in marked contrast to the ersatz Mughal creation by John Nash that superseded it. (Imagine Jimmy the Mod in *Quadrophenia* a couple of years on taking a hit of acid on the Prom and trading in his drainpipes and neat jacket 'cut slim and checkered' for a Kaftan and a pair of velvet loons, and we are possibly near the spot, comparison-wise.)

Installing Mrs Fitzherbert in her own house nearby, the Prince left London in July 1786, and remained loyal to Brighton, with the odd lapses, of course, for the next forty years. When it came for the Prince to do his duty and marry for the good of the nation and his bank balance, Caroline of Brunswick, a woman who repulsed him, the honeymoon was in Brighton. Having fortified himself with brandy he was, however, too drunk to consummate the union on their first night together in the Pavilion, the deed only being fulfilled the following morning. It is perhaps more apt than usual then that Caroline should be honoured by a pub in the town. On its sign today, George's sexually incontinent, fat and notoriously unhygienic spouse, is depicted, with blithe indifference to such historical detail, as a buxom cartoon vamp. A right royal Jessica Rabbit, whose ample charms struggle to remain within the bounds of some tight fitting red robes, she winks lasciviously at passing trade on the Ditchling Road. In next door Hove, however, her family name does grace the prime Georgian estate of Brunswick Town, a terrace and square of stately clotted cream stucco and black iron-railed buildings that abut the seafront.

Sex, inebriation, retiring from the capital and dubiously funded property: so many of the recurring leitmotifs of Brighton, and plenty of other seaside resorts in its wake, can be traced back to George's day.

Like Oliver Postgate's saggy old cloth cat Bagpuss, with his attendant crew of organ mice, knitted toads, manikins and wooden bookends, the Prince, especially during those formative years in the town, had the power to rally the place into life. And correspondingly, whenever he and his entourage of hangers-on departed, it went back to sleep again. Noting his absence at one point in 1784, the *Brighthelmstone Intelligence* reported that 'within these last few days [Brighton] has become a desert; scarce a person of fashion remains; the whole company now consists of antiquated virgins, emaciated beaux, and wealthy citizens with their wives and daughters.' On his return, however, suddenly all, they claimed, was 'alive and merry here'. And merry, where the Prince and some of his circle were concerned, was the word. His presence, while attracting the cream of the *beau monde*, brought with it the dregs of the demi, too. Though they were frequently indistinguishable.

Just as in more recent times seemingly every public school-educated mover and shaker lost their cut-class vowels, befriended gangsters and gained a love of football, the late eighteenth and early nineteenth century was equally marked by a mania for class tourism and elegant slumming. Swaggering about in pantaloons, chewing the fat about 'the Fancy' and pretending to be an expert in horseflesh were all de rigueur among youthful nobles around this period – and many of those around the Prince, in particular.

Perhaps the most dissolute of his associates to visit him in Brighton were Sir John Lade, heir to a vast brewing fortune whose wife Letitia counted the highwayman 'Sixteen-stringed Jack' as an ex-lover; the Duke of Norfolk, a soap dodging dipsomaniac; the Duke of Queensbury, a Hellfire Club member and opera and racing fanatic and the Barrymores – a clan whose eccentric characteristics were set out in their respective nicknames. Richard, the 7th Earl, was a competent jockey known as Hellgate for his wildness. His younger brother the Hon. Henry had a club foot and so was called Cripplegate, while the Rev. Augustus was a compulsive gambler forever on the verge of imprisonment and accordingly dubbed Newgate, after the gaol. And their sister Lady Caroline had such a fruity tongue that Prinny himself christened her Billingsgate.

Known as 'the outstanding bucks in the flashiest crowd at Brighton', the Barrymore brothers were especially fond of high japes. You instinctively feel that had they lived in an age when donning a Nazi uniform for a fancy dress party was in any way a possibility, they would have done it. The direct biological forerunners of the toffs in deck shoes to be seen cutting it loose in modern day north Cornwall, they delighted in uprooting as many signs as they could on the pelt down from London. Once in the town, they would tour

Brighton with a coffin, terrifying housemaids by knocking on doors and offering to bury the dead, a stunt that appears a premonition of the spooky ghost rides later to be found on the front. (And, more morbidly, perhaps, an omen of Richard Barrymore's own premature death. He died at twenty-four, shot through the eye when a loaded pistol he was carrying in his carriage went off accidentally.)

Horses, hunting, shooting, gambling, the odd showgirl and some forays into the world of neo-Classical architecture: the pleasures of the nobility sometimes look scarcely altered in over three hundred years. But those predilections are surely also reflected in the shooting galleries, merry-go-rounds and fruit machines of our seaside amusements. Which, much like sandcastles, are after all only mini-me versions of the hunting lodges, stables and clubland gambling tables that the better sorts always had access to.

That said, the Prince of Wales himself seems something of a pioneer of arcade-style shoot-it-up games. Mrs Creevey, wife of the Whig statesman Thomas, gives a first hand account of a rather boisterous evening with the Prince at the Pavilion in a letter to her husband in October 1805. Strikingly, the Prince's festivities seem like a microcosm of 1001 out-of-hand seaside jaunts ever since.

Mrs Creevey begins by complaining, in almost Bridget Jones fashion, that a headache has kept her in bed until midday. 'My head is very bad, I suppose,' she writes, 'with the heat of the Pavilion last night.' Others, you suspect, from what she goes on to outline, might be feeling a good deal worse – and not from heat alone. When the Prince first appeared, Creevey notes that she 'instantly saw he had got more wine than usual.' More wine than usual? This, about an heir to the throne who could possibly have given Oliver Reed a run for his money. The Prince then 'led all the party . . . to see him shoot an air gun at a target placed at the end of the room.' Despite his inebriated state, he apparently, 'did it very skilfully' From then on things start to get out of hand: '[H]e wanted all the ladies to attempt it. The girls and I excused ourselves on account of our short sight, but Lady Downshire hit a fiddler in the dining room, Miss Johnstone a door, and Bloomfield the ceiling . . .' Finally the band struck a waltz, bringing a halt to any further devastation. The Prince, clasping Miss Johnstone to him, proceeded to dance around the table. After a single lap however, he became too giddy to continue.

Such antics, naturally enough, earned the Prince and his cohorts the stern disapproval of the press. 'Morning rides, champagne, dissipation, noise, nonsense: jumble these phrases together, and you have a complete account of all that's passing at Brighthelmstone', thundered one quite early dispatch from the *Morning Post* in July 1785. 'Women of virtue and character shun these scenes of debauchery and drunkenness', it stated just a month later. Spying the number of 'idle, sauntering land-lubbers' swanning about the place dressed in 'buff trousers' and 'slight jackets', their reporter, outrage itself, found himself wishing 'for a sturdy press gang any morning on the Steyne to give them useful employment or at least keep them out of mischief.'

One might almost imagine that the declaration of war with France in February 1793 would therefore have pleased the *Morning Post*. As the entry point for the Continent offering the shortest possible overland route from the English Channel to London, Brighton had been a point of arrival and departure for France. Now, it was vulnerable to attack and garrisons of infantrymen were soon billeted in the town. A barracks was built close to the Pavilion, and the Prince of Wales, commanding his favourite regiment the 10th Light Dragoons, threw himself into the mock battles that were practised on Belle Vue Fields near the front.

But if the *Post* believed that the arrival of military drill would clean up the town, they were sorely mistaken. Soldiers only added to the rakishness of the place.[7] For the likes of Lydia in *Pride and Prejudice*, they far outweighed the Prince or even the sea as the resort's liveliest attraction. 'In Lydia's imagination', Austen writes, 'a visit to Brighton comprised every possibility of earthly happiness. She saw, with the creative eye of fancy, the streets of that gay bathing place covered with officers. She saw herself the object of attention to tens and to scores of them at present unknown. She saw all the glories of the camp; its tents stretched forth in beauteous uniformity of lines, crowded with the young and the gay, and dazzling with scarlet; and to complete the view, she saw herself seated beneath a tent, tenderly flirting with at least six officers at once.'[8]

Later deflowered by Mr Wickham, an officer but no gentlemen who is paid to marry her, Lydia is almost as

---

7 With access to the Continent blocked for much of this period, blades who might have sown youthful oats without disgrace in the fleshpots of Paris or Rome were forced to make do with the English coasts.

8 The soldiers certainly added to the Gayness of Brighton in other lasting respects too. In August 1822, a guardsman accused George Wilson, a servant from Newcastle he'd met in the Duke of Wellington pub in Pool Valley, of offering him two sovereign and two shillings to go to the beach and 'commit an unnatural crime.'

good as a prostitute to Austen. However, during the period in which the novel was set, there were estimated to be 'a Cyprian corps' of over three hundred actual whores attending to the needs of the servicemen in the town. Also referred to as 'French milliners' – an easily decipherable euphemism that rather neatly combines eternal English preconceptions about sex and our cross-Channel neighbours with a profession that gives heads good wear – prostitutes had been flocking to Brighton from the moment the Prince and his cohorts adopted the town. Since a greater number of the 'gentlemen of fancy' were now to be discovered cutting it up on the coast in the summer months than in the pleasure gardens of Ranelagh or in the bordellos of Covent Garden – then the capital's premier quarter of sin – this was simply a matter of professional prudence.

Their ubiquity on the Brighton scene is confirmed in satirical drawings from the era by the likes of John Nixon. Nixon was a successful merchant and pursued his art as an amateur, in the true sense of that word. A friend and pupil of Rowlandson, whose scabrous style he emulates, his watercolour and ink sketch 'Picture Morning: Amusements at Brighton' currently hangs in the Museum and Art Gallery in Pavilion Gardens. Showing a beach awash with warp-framed bathing contraptions, scabby trollops, wan invalids and gouty pleasure seekers, it is a picture that should really have dissuaded all but the most syphilitic from visiting.

But by the time George assumed the Regency in 1811, Brighthelmstone's population had swollen to over 7,000. The Regent, who seemed to have expanded in unison with the resort, was himself now a corpulent *roué* of nearly fifty with a waist in inches that exceeded his age in years. Observed imbibing around three bottles of wine plus spirits with most evening meals and with prodigious laudanum intake to boot, the Prince had become so ridden with gout he frequently had to be wheeled around the Pavilion in a Merlin chair. Rather like a less vicious Stalin in the Kremlin or possibly a jumpsuit-wearing Elvis at Gracelands, within the confines of this inner sanctum by the sea, he grew ever more tyrannical about indulging his own whims.

Guests had to be particularly alert to his needs and moods. Recently purchased treasures were brought out only to be admired. The dinner gong that he kept time with on musical nights needed to be saluted as a boon to any piece played. And the German military bands he cherished had to be applauded through every headache inducing cymbal crash. While tales of prowess on the battlefield (fantasies embellished, much like the Pavilion itself, with every passing year) were never to be questioned too closely. But perhaps it's easier to lose track of reality when you are strung out on opium, ensconced in Oriental splendour and, after Bonaparte's defeat, the head of a coming Imperial power. And Nash's Mughal-style Pavilion seems about the most decorative, or dreamlike, instantiation of the nation's surging trading interests one could wish for.

Derided in its day as a 'gilded dirt pie', a 'minaret mushroom' and a 'congeries of bulbous excrescences', the Royal Pavilion is an almost breathtakingly sacrilegious twist on Islamic religious architecture. Not unlike curried beef say, or the lard and tallow greased bullets for the Enfield rifles that helped trigger (no pun intended) the Indian Mutiny, it is a confection that only the British could possibly have mustered with a straight face.[9] Soon even the Prince had tired of it and Brighton, breathing his last in dreary old Windsor in 1830. The arrival of the railway in 1841, greeted with protests locally, further stripped Brighton of its regality. But correspondingly increased its availability to ordinary working folk, who soaked up its raffish airs in their own way. Christian evangelism, however, had by then gripped the land. The bowdlerisers of Shakespeare and a mercantile middle class that placed a greater value on probity, were in the ascendancy. The late George, *enfant terrible* and aged embarrassment, became a potent symbol of all that had been rotten in the House of Hanover. The Royal Pavilion a byword for gaudy excess. If William IV remained loyal to Brighton, Victoria put some clear blue water between herself and her predecessors by dragging Albert and the kids off to Osborne House on the Isle of Wight at the earliest opportunity.

And this was the thing. Newly democratised by the railways, the seaside, once a terrain of adult entertainments,

---

9 When last visited, it was undergoing substantial renovations, which only added to the perversity of its appearance. Its main domes were obscured by complex arrangements of wood and metal bars. Their tips poked out from these fixtures like the nipples of a strip joint dancer in bondage gear. (Or so I imagine . . .) The Regent's baroque *chinoiserie* interior is almost a parody of gaudy excess: shades of red, yellow, green, pink, shiny black ornaments, gilt finishes, richly embossed fabrics, figurines, wall-spanning Chinese dragons, serpents and tree fronds all vie for attention. It's sublime *and* ridiculous. Though barely discernible when surrounded by its all-encompassing Oriental exoticism, the experience of moving inside is perhaps rather like walking into your local Taj Mahal takeaway and finding Sweet and Sour Won Ton and Crab Foo Yung on the menu. It is a sort of fusion style, perhaps, centuries before the term was bandied around by TV chefs.

was becoming more about . . . the family. The aquariums and souvenir shell shops that sprung up were a testament to the emerging Victorians' pedagogical and materialist impulses. Brighton moved with those times, adding the earliest electric railway in Britain, Volks, to its family-orientated gimcracks. But it could still be romanticised, much like Lord Byron, as terribly naughty. And it has remained the quintessential destination for a dirty weekend. Seedy enough to be seemly but carefree enough not to comment, and imitated up and down the coasts of the land.

3
We Are Not Amused

*We Are Not Amused – On Track for the Coast
– Without Pier – Cooking Up the Bank Holiday –
Paleontology, Pierrots & Mr Punch – Stop Me & Buy
One – Towering Over Lancashire, Shot in Sussex*

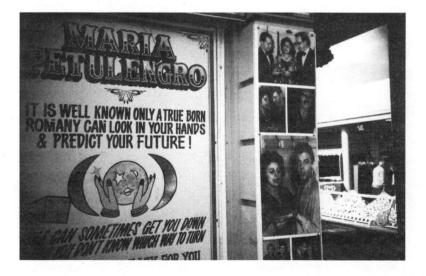

It was in the 1980s, a decade presided over by a government committed to laissez-faire economics and fond of
espousing the moral worth of self-reliance and a return
to so-called Victorian values, that Jimmy Saville fronted
an advertising campaign for British Rail that maintained,
'This is the age of the train.' Sadly, such a claim proved, as it
happened, to be so widely off the mark it seems almost pitiable today. A century and a half earlier, however, England
had been in the grip of a railway mania that can more
genuinely be said to have epitomised an age. And over the
course of Victoria's reign, it was the country's engineering
prowess, coupled with a growing fondness for subjugating
indigenous peoples and a less than benign interest in the
opium trade, that helped to transform Britain into a global
Imperial power.

Closer to home and our subject, the steam locomotive
engine was not only to radically alter the nation's landscape
and perceptions of geography, it also imposed an entirely
new sense of time on the nation.

Before 1840, when the Great Western Railway first
sought to standardise all the clocks on its lines, a scheme
that was fiercely resisted in some quarters for the next
fifty years, Britain had operated on a hotchpotch of
different, regional time zones. A journey from one
place to another could, at least feasibly, involve arriving before you'd left. When the cycles of the seasons and
availability of daylight hours continued to hold sway
over most businesses and all means of transport were
powered by a horse or a sail, such temporal ebbs and
flows were of little importance. But the mechanisation
of labour, travel and even time itself, as far more reliable

and durable timepieces came into being, made greater standardisation increasingly inevitable. In this newly industrial society, time was money. The shifting sands of the hourglass and the flickering shadows of the sundial were permanently cast aside in favour of the chimes of Big Ben (and think how many classic Victorian buildings are dominated by their clock towers), the rigours of the railway timetable and the teleological peaks and troughs of profit and loss reports.

And of course, the same sooty technological kit that would ultimately bring the seaside within easier reach of the poorest elements of society was simultaneously enslaving them to fifteen-hour-days of robotic factory toil. This business of doing business more efficiently proved remarkably proficient at stripping artisans and office workers alike of traditional rest days, feasts and pitchfork-and-pen-downing opportunities.

Today we take it for granted that there is a 'holiday industry' and perhaps fail to realise just how significant the latter word is, or was. The process of industrialisation was accompanied by an intensive urbanisation that saw over half the population of Britain living in major towns and cities by the point of Wordsworth's death in 1850. And it was the grimy squalor of the everyday environment that plainly made the seaside seem an ever more appealing destination for put-upon urban dwellers. That the basic idling rights and common lands of repair of the lowliest had been severely curtailed over the course of a few decades only increased its desirability.

Rather like the fallow field in the crop rotation system of feudal farming, the trip to the seaside would become an almost intrinsic part of the cycle of industrial production. Although only acknowledged extremely begrudgingly and after some hard bargaining by reforming campaigners who succeeded in passing the Factory Acts of the 1840s, it was gradually accepted by employers that the odd day away from the loom – and especially ones spent out of the metropolis, with its smoky pubs and dodgy gaming houses – far from damaging profitability, could enhance it. But in coming to perform its function as 'the lungs' of London or the mill towns of Lancashire, the coast was itself heavily industrialised, again, in ways that we've largely ceased to register.

Your classic seaside pier, all wooden decking and curly ironwork, appears positively bucolic nowadays. Only a little off a two hundred foot long lobster pot adorned with fruity machines, say. I am exaggerating, obviously. But it's perhaps easy to forget the advances in engineering needed to build them and what an imposition on the existing scenery these structures represented to begin with. In John Constable's 'The Chain Pier', his 1827 painting of the earliest pier at Brighton, we have a period document that provides a quite startling reminder of how strangely forbidding – or just how strange – they possibly were. To Constable, at the very least.

Beneath a malevolent sky of chewy blue-grey clouds, the Chain Pier is depicted as a knotty tendril in the distance. It could be a row of electricity pylons or some tin megasaurus having a dip in the water. Framed to the left by rows of lofty townhouses and below by a foreshore of cresting sludgy waves, dirty brown sand, drift wood, sail boats, fishermen and the odd dog, it genuinely does look other-worldly, distinctly, almost menacingly, alien in fact. There is a hint of the Martian craft in H.G. Wells's *War of the Worlds* about it. Or if you are of a certain age, a touch of the leggy metal Tripods from the BBC TV sci-fi series of the same name.

The Chain Pier had only been erected four years before Constable committed it to canvas – in the same year, incidentally, that the Old Steine, an area of common land up from the front, was enclosed, although retained as a public park, and the salty lags who for generations had fixed their boats and nets there were evicted.

Utilising some of the most recent technical advances, the Pier was built along the lines of a suspension bridge. As structural forms go, few could be more symbolic of the tireless spirit of early nineteenth-century British engineering, the era when the world belonged to mutton-chop whiskered men like Isambard Kingdom Brunel.

The Chain Pier's designer, Captain Samuel Brown, was a similarly impressive character. A naval commander turned architectural engineer who 'owing to some injury or defect . . . walked somewhat limping with the assistance of a stick', Brown had previously introduced iron cables to the Royal Navy and overseen the construction of the Union suspension bridge over the Tweed. The Chain, at 340 yards long and 13 feet wide and planked with a pitched Norwegian fir wood, didn't go 'over' anything as such, merely jutted out into the English Channel. 'Here for the sum of twopence', wrote Thackeray, admiringly, 'you can go out to sea and pace this vast deck without the need of a basin.'

And this was, and remains, an enduring part of the allure

of piers. With the waters swirling beneath you and wind and spray in your face, you are offered all the sensuality of an ocean voyage without the fear of drowning, seasickness, scurvy, etc. With a head full of lines from Byron's *The Corsair*

> O'er the glad waters of the dark blue sea,
> Our thoughts as boundless, and our souls as free,
> Far as the breeze can bear, the billows foam,
> Survey our empire, and behold our home!

you could hobble up and down the planking, much like its architect, perhaps, playing at pirates.

Romanticism aside, though, the Chain Pier was commissioned as a practical landing stage for cross-Channel vessels. As the consortium of local businessmen who funded its creation maintained in their prospectus, its purpose was to 'greatly increase the attractions of Brighton as a place of fashionable resort, and multiply its local advantages as a point of transit to the coast of France.' It was in this role that it accommodated a young Queen Victoria and her Prince Consort as they disembarked from an early State tour of Europe. This in itself would prove a rare visit to Brighton by the monarch, who disliked the place.

If we consider 'the Pier' an almost quintessential feature of the Victorian seaside, and a complete archetype of the English seaside in general, as surely we do, this is perhaps apt, since Ryde on the Isle of Wight has long staked a claim to possessing one of the earliest piers in Britain. As the historian John Walton notes in *British Piers*, in the nineteenth century, the Isle of Wight 'positively bristled with piers' possessing seven by 1895. But even at this late stage, little distinction was made between a pier of the iron finger of fun type and a pier that was hardly more than a mooring point. And on an island that is only accessible from the mainland by boat, the latter were predominant, with the original Ryde Pier, built in wood and opening in 1818, falling closer to that category. By then, in any case, the stone jetty at Margate, which received steam boats full of cockneys from up the Thames, had already acquired some of the accoutrements of pierdom, including a gallery where bands played, peddlers and a promenade that cost a penny to stroll along.

Nevertheless, Brighton's Chain Pier was a significant advance on either of these earlier propositions. Not least in being twice as expensive as Margate at the toll booth, a measure designed to keep it socially exclusive. Once the railways began to bring an ever wider mix of sorts to the country's beaches and promenades, that kind of segregation would become a valuable attraction in itself. Piers from then on were built and promoted as signs of civic prestige and competition over them was as politely fierce as at any game of cricket or flower show. (The English may dislike showiness but they are still keen to show they are better than their neighbours.)

The Chain, though, was purposely grand from its inception. Its supporting towers aped Egyptian obelisks. (During the period of the pier's construction, the Rosetta Stone, essentially a spoil from Nelson's victory at the Battle of the Nile, was being deciphered in the British Museum.) These were either fashioned with room for little shops at their feet at the outset or they were adapted to that purpose soon afterwards.[10] Before finally being destroyed, 'amidst general regret, by the fearful storm of December 4th, 1896', the Chain had numbered a reading room, telescopes and a camera obscura among its facilities and it played host to firework displays, vendors of souvenirs, specialists in wax flowers, silhouette artists, and more latterly, daguerreotype and glass plate photographers.

Like the Pier itself, such diversions were no less representative of industrialisation and Imperial exchange. China trinkets mass-produced in Staffordshire were soon staples of any Victorian seaside kiosk. And as Maureen Duffy observes in *England: The Making of the Myth*, in a culture devoted to trade, the sailor, as the principle agent of any imports and exports, was to gain an additional patriotic edge. The fashion for dressing up young children in sailor's suits, inspired by the gift of a scaled-down uniform to the four-year-old future Edward VII on the Royal Yacht in 1846, was highly symbolic. By 1900, half the ships on the high seas were registered in Britain and a third of world trade was controlled by the country. To stride on the planking of a pier, gander at the waves and possibly do a little shopping was, in a sense, then to affirm all that was supposedly making the nation great. Equally, to build something that stretched out into the surrounding waters was almost

10 The first department stores, a potent indicator of the arrival of a new mercantile middle class and of shopping as an established leisure pursuit, appeared in the 1830s. The Reform Bill of 1832, which gave the vote to 'ten pound householders', had tacitly acknowledged their growing importance too, whilst also seeking to align the interests of property owners, or those that aspired to it, with the landed gentry. And after 1859, when the East India Company was transferred to the crown, England really did become a nation of shopkeepers.

to assert rights to those oceans themselves. Or certainly to imply that the boundaries of the country were amorphous to say the least. Rather like a homeowner cheekily taking a few inches off a neighbour's garden while building a new wall, it was a gesture of proprietorial self-importance.

As piers became ever more elaborate, gaining the minarets and domes that characterise a quasi-Eastern seaside aesthetic that is part cricket clubhouse and part *Alice in Wonderland* whimsy, stirring thoughts of the pink bits on the map were almost unavoidable. All the spiked ironwork of that period was, as Jonathan Raban once put it, another reminder of 'the teeth of Imperial capitalism'. And, naturally, the technology that underpinned much of that decorative frippery itself hailed from the railways and the Empire, further underscoring what a quite uniquely English phenomenon the pier is.

If suspension bridges had Brunel, the canals Brindley, the railways Watt and Stephenson and the sewers, Bazalgette, then seaside piers had Eugenius Birch – the engineer responsible for fourteen of them around England and Wales and a veteran of the Calcutta-Delhi railway who also designed the docks at Exmouth, Ilfracombe harbour and the West Surrey Waterworks. Aberystwyth, Deal, Hornsea, Lytham, Plymouth, New Brighton, Eastbourne, Scarborough, Weston-Super-Mare, Hastings and Bournemouth all sported Birch piers in their prime.

Birch's unique contribution to pier-ing was the cast-iron screw pile. Before he entered the field, the decking of any pier, Brown's suspension model included, rested upon a series of wooden posts, which were simply hammered into the ground. His screw pile, however, fixed, *screwed*, as you might expect, the supports firmly into the seabed. This innovation revolutionised pier building. Not only did it make their construction largely a matter of assembly – and in time even prefabricated kits were available, the seafronts at Clevedon and Morecambe acquired off-the-shelf piers in the late 1860s – it also made them far more stable and durable. In Brighton, virtually all that now survives of the West Pier, one of Birch's earliest but finest efforts, are its screw piles. Reduced to a decrepit skeleton by arsonist fires in 2003, these metal foundations now poke up through the waves like the legs of a long dead spider.

Featuring an expansive open-decked promenade four times wider than that offered by the Chain Pier, Italianate toll booths, Oriental kiosks and an ingenious, and much imitated, arrangement of raised double seats, shielded by ornamental plate glass and iron weather screens that one early commentator believed would not 'fail to be productive of a great comfort to the frequenters of the pier' especially as it would allow invalids on sunny wintry days to 'enjoy the mild temperature and life-prolonging air with the perfect freedom from chilling blasts', the West Pier was a kind of Bentley of the beach. (That use of the word 'productive' is so tellingly Victorian.)

Set to the west of the Steine and directly opposite Regency Square, one of the most distinguished slices of late-Georgian real estate in the town, its locality was almost as important as its design and facilities. And its location angered some local residents, who feared their sea views were being compromised and that it might attract undesirables. In the event, an admittance fee that reached a positively extortionate six pence in 1875, a dress code that lasted until the 1930s and an imposing pair of entrance gates and turnstiles kept things pretty select, despite notching up over 600,000 admissions a year in its late-Victorian heyday. At a point when the better off travelled by carriage to avoid the scrum (and scum) of the streets, a good promenade was prized and could attract such a premium, precisely because it reversed the normal order of the roads.

Unlike its near neighbour, the West Pier was never intended to be a landing stage as such. Though its head was adapted to receive pleasure steamers in the Edwardian era, it opened in 1866 when the majority of visitors to Brighton were being carried there by rail and its importance as a departure point for the Continent had also waned.

Arriving in 1841, the railway itself had met considerable resistance in Brighton but it ensured its long-term survival: within ten years the population had risen from 46,000 to 65,000.

Elsewhere the effects of the railway were equally dramatic. Only a year earlier, Fleetwood, a newly established port a few miles from Blackpool was reached by the Preston and Wyre railway. Within a month, thousands were streaming into Fleetwood and heading on down into the neighbouring, and until that point, fairly top drawer resort. 'The town', one Bolton newspaper observed, 'swarms with human beings . . . The Fleetwood and Wyre railroad seems to have contributed to this extraordinary influx of visitors'. Eleven years later, and five years after the line had been extended to Blackpool itself, the *Preston Pilot* was complaining that 'unless cheap trains are discontinued or some effective regulation made . . . Blackpool as a resort for respectable visitors will be ruined.'

The permanent way, though, was here for good. And, thanks to Gladstone's Railway Act of 1844, a piece of legislation that compelled train companies to provide safer, cheap carriages for the less well off, more accessible than ever. They might have been resented or resisted by the likes of Scarborough and Weymouth – both towns, elder statesmen in the pantheon of coastal resorts, waged Canute-like battles to keep trains at bay, hanging out until 1845 and 1857, respectively – but no amount of harping on about the lowering of tones or scaremongering about the arrival of vagrants could ultimately disguise the commercial gains that being on the rail network, (more of a cobweb back then perhaps) could bring.

The former minnow Blackpool might have lost some of its nobler patrons but it doubled in size within a decade of the railway's arrival. While Rhyl, a coastal hamlet of just two buildings in 1800, found itself on the line from Chester to Holyhead in 1848 and within a mere four years had swelled into a watering spot of over two hundred lodging houses. In the case of Cleethorpes in Lincolnshire, the railway company financed the construction of the pier and a pleasure gardens, including a picturesque ruined folly. Little wonder then, that the opening of the train station in way-out-west Torquay was marked by a day's holiday locally.

As one contemporary commentator reflected, 'men who but a few years since scarcely crossed the precincts of the county in which they were born and knew as little of the general feature of the land of their birth as they did the topography of the moon, now unhesitatingly avail themselves of the communications that are afforded' (i.e. jump on a train and explore the country for themselves).

And if any single event can really be said to have incul-
cated the nation at large into 'the railway habit', the Great
Exhibition of 1851 was it. This monumental, Imperial
chest-thumping jamboree at Hyde Park, housed in Joseph
Paxton's astonishing 'Crystal Palace', attracted over six
million 'visits' and bequeathed an idea of the quasi-
educational spectacle that would have lasting consequence
for the seaside resort. Its special cut-price 'Shilling Days'
drew trippers from across the land; famously (or possibly
fictionally) the eighty-four-year-old Mary Callinan walked
all the way from Penzance, clutching just a single coin for
the entrance fee in her hand. But it was the new excursion
trains that did most to pack the punters in.

Some 165,000 people were ferried to London for the
Exhibition in engines booked through the travel agent
Thomas Cook. Cook was possibly an unlikely found-
ing father of the cheap package deal, a type of holiday
now almost synonymous with Brits-On-the-Piss in Spain.
He was a committed temperance campaigner. Acting as
Secretary to the South Midland Temperance Association,
he was the author of numerous morally uplifting anti-
drink pamphlets and founder in 1840 of the *Children's
Temperance Magazine*, a publication that even with
five-year-old kiddies then supping gin in the pubs, must
surely have struggled against the latest outings by Captain
Marayat or Hans Christian Andersen.

A wood turner by trade, Cook had ventured into the
travel game after organising an outing from Leicester to
a temperance fete in Loughborough in July 1841. Various
Sunday School parties and, at the other end of the spec-
trum, racegoers had hired trains for jaunts before him.

Cook, however, is thought to be the first person to act as a fully fledged agent, coughing up for the train and then going out and seeking passengers separately. In this first instance, five hundred and seventy soft-drink-loving souls, who each paid a shilling for the trip – food included. By 1872, Cook would be offering a round-the-world tour for £210. But on the home front, the excursions he inaugurated in the 1840s to spots of natural interest such as the Lake District, Snowdon and Loch Lomond in Scotland and to Fleetwood and Blackpool on the Lancashire coast – beanos that still mixed pleasure with a self-improving appreciation of the scenic – laid the foundations for the type of days out that would become annual rituals for many after the passing of the Bank Holiday Act in 1871.

This Act, which in the words of John Walton, 'tapped the enormous national potential for leisure', was the brainchild of Sir John Lubbock. A classic frock-coated philanthropist, Lubbock was a banker, cricket fan and the Liberal MP for Maidstone, who had grown up with Charles Darwin as a near neighbour and, spurred on by the evolutionist, went on to write several books on the natural sciences and anthropology himself. As a parliamentarian he was behind a slew of progressive measures that included securing a reduction of the working week to 74 hours for shop staff. But the Bank Holiday Act would remain his finest, and wiliest, contribution to the statute book.

In focussing squarely on the rights of banking staff, those inky-fingered ledger-keeping Bob Cratchetts who, in terms of holidays, had fared as badly – if not worse – than the Stephen Blackpools in the mills or factories in the fallout from industrialisation, Lubbock, in a sense, pulled off an adroit piece of misdirection. For what the finished Act enshrined was the provision of universal holidays at Christmas, New Year, Easter, Whit Monday and the first Monday in August. And while in the two decades that elapsed between the Great Exhibition and Lubbock's Act, the numbers of those visiting the seaside thanks to the railways had risen exponentially, the influx now unleashed took almost everyone by surprise. On the inaugural August Bank Holiday of 1871, the *News of the World* reported that Fenchurch Street and Charing Cross stations in London had been inundated by huge crowds of would-be-excursionists. Although railway officials had succeeded in purloining an additional seven trains from Cannon Street and 'as many more from Highgate Hill' to run 'specials' to the coasts, they were still unable to meet the demand for tickets to Margate, Southend and Ramsgate.

Such scenes were now repeated year on year, and the arrival of the hoi polloi at certain cherished watering places was greeted with dismay by many of their wealthier seasonal residents. Some responded by choosing to holiday at different times of the year or elsewhere: the Continent, now that the revolutions of 1848 had slipped into memory, rose in allure once again. But in a stratified society where the classes existed as virtually parallel castes, rank firmly delineated by the bells you could tug or the doors you might enter by, much more subtle divisions could be preserved in loosely the same geographical space. Think of the layers of coloured sand in a souvenir from Alum Bay and we are not far off the mark.

Arguably, Victorian seaside resorts were not that much more egalitarian than the major towns or cities, with their eastern slums and wealthier west ends, say. And in the larger resorts, districts like the North Shore in Blackpool and the South Bay at Scarborough saw themselves – and were seen – as the preserve of 'the better sort', while the South Shore and North Bay, respectively, embraced the less well-heeled. But as with attendance at the Great Exhibition, there was a sense that the seaside was now available for everyone, from Queen Victoria on the Isle of Wight to a Manchester garment worker on a day trip to Fleetwood. And at some resorts all human life was quite genuinely there. Though, as the Tuggs family in Dickens's *Sketches by Boz,* who reject Gravesend as 'LOW' and Margate as 'worse and worse – nobody there, but tradespeople', before finally settling on Ramsgate, had already illustrated back in 1836, exactly where you watered in England would always remain a question of class. (George and Weedon Grossmith's self-important Charles Pooter might roll up at Dickens's own watering place, Broadstairs, but his decision to bag 'very nice apartments by the station' rather than ones on the cliff at 'double the price' reveal him to be a man of no importance.)

What you did (or didn't) do, however, was no less important than where you went. Preserved in the rather pathetic nylon shrimping nets to be found on sale in beach shacks almost everywhere today, taking an active interest in the flora and fauna of the seashore was certainly one means of demonstrating superiority on the coast. Encouraged by the writings of Philip Gosse, marine biology duly became a popular hobby among middle-class Victorians and the more autodidactic of working-class visitors.

In that somewhat uncharitable if still captivating memoir, *Father and Son,* Edmund Gosse complains that many of the habitats in Devon that his father held most dear were irreparably damaged by the legions of overeager admirers who, in homage, sought to conduct field studies of their own. However true that might have been, the vogue for natural sciences was not stoked by his father's works alone but fitted in with a wider taste for classification and identification among the Victorians. It can be seen in the documentation of the London poor undertaken by Mayhew, as much as in the fossil collecting of Elizabeth Philpott. And as William Dyce's 'Pegwell Bay' (1858), (a rather tidy portrait of a family group, all Little Alices in petticoats and Master Alberts in round-collars foraging amid the rock pools and chalky cliffs of this Kentish resort) illustrates, on the eve of the publication of Darwin's *On the Origin of Species,* fossil hunting was a highly respectable beach pursuit.

It was Disraeli who famously maintained that Britain in his day was a country of two nations, but a more general kind of contrary duality seems to run through the culture at large wherever you look. As the narrator of John Fowles's *The French Lieutenant's Woman*, (a novel where an upper-crust palaeontologist falls for a governess ostracised in flinty Victorian Lyme for dallying with a less than gallant Gallic in Weymouth) comments, there was an 'endless tug of war between Liberty and Restraint, Excess and Moderation, Propriety and Conviction'. At seaside resorts, as perhaps the locale of Fowles's tale might indicate, these binaries seem to come into even sharper relief.

On Victorian seafronts – home, by the 1870s, to aquariums and phrenologists, shell shops and mass-market souvenir vendors, botanical gardens and funfairs, photographers and magicians, palm readers and newsboys, semi-nude (for the period) bathers and smartly uniformed German bands, temperance campaigners and beer halls, minstrels and preachers – science and superstition, nature and artifice, education and entertainment, God and Mammon, carefree contemplation and hard commerce and activity and indolence, were all to be found jockeying for position.

As Darwinian theories of evolution began to eat away at some of the most cherished religious certainties, fantasy would become increasingly appealing, necessary possibly. (What else explains the late-Victorian predilection for making railway stations – and even seaside hotels and aquariums, for that matter – look like medieval churches? The one was the stand-in for the other.) Escapism, though, is a much more obvious leitmotif of the seaside in the final years of Victoria's lengthy reign. In addition to Bank Holidays and cheaper transport, the cost of basic commodities fell, allowing even those with quite limited resources to exercise far more consumer choices than ever before. And those whose daily lives, by necessity, were most rigidly frugal were, arguably, possibly more susceptible to the entreaties to spend that resorts now provided.

Bands of musicians, peddlers, tumblers and jugglers and quack doctors had, of course, long fished for coins on the beaches. Back in 1847 Charles Dickens had complained that the incessant noise from the entertainers on the sands below his summer house at Broadstairs, a cacophony of the 'most excruciating organs, fiddles, bells or glee-singers', made it impossible for him to write there unless it rained. And one of the earliest, if most dubious, American entries into the field of English seaside amusements, the

'Nigger' Minstrels, were already a common sight in British resorts just over a decade later. The craze for 'black-face' entertainment troupes, one that lasted until the three-day-week and Hughie Green, if not even, disappointingly, slightly beyond that, was kicked off by the American music hall star Thomas Dartmouth 'Daddy' Rice in the 1830s. Inspired, or so the story goes, by the sight of a crippled slave, Rice had adopted the stage persona of, what at best could be described as a physically-challenged black rustic and at worst . . . doesn't really bear thinking about. The 'highlight' of his act was a song entitled 'Jump Jim Crow', a number that was performed, if the surviving pen and ink drawings of Rice in action are to be believed, with all the racial sensitivity its title implies.

But with new theatres, music halls, bandstands, piers, ballrooms and winter gardens such as Blackpool's (opening in 1875 and designed to hold over 6,000 people) springing up to capture some of the extra money sloshing around, the range of diversions to be had at the seaside expanded exponentially. By the close of the century the minstrels themselves (for the most part, officially sanctioned roving players who worked beach pitches with concertinas, banjos and whistles) were facing some stiff competition from their counterpoints in greasepaint, the Pierrots. Another import, though this time from across the Channel, the first Pierrot group in Britain was established by the banjo player and musical impresario Clifford Essex in 1891. Essex had become entranced by the Pierrots in French pantomimes, earlier interlopers to Parisian theatre from Italian *commedia dell'arte*, on a trip to France and promptly lifted their clownish get-up (white make-up, ruff-necked tunics, bobbly hats, and baggy pants etc.) for his busking band. The Clifford Essex Pierrots (later the Royal Pierrots) debuted at Henley Regatta, serenading crowds from a punt, before heading to Ryde and Sandown on the Isle of Wight for the first of what proved to be twenty-three consecutive summer seasons.

As their opening association with Henley perhaps suggests, the Pierrots were considered a tad more refined and therefore more family friendly than the Minstrels. Though many former minstrels, including the acclaimed Victorian banjoist Joe Morley, merely swapped burnt cork for flour and carried on, with troupes such as Will Pepper's White Coons, fixtures in Felixstowe for many years, somehow conspiring to preserve what was most offensive about their original act in a new incarnation. And one of the curious features of the late-nineteenth-century resort is that they became both more sensational and technically sophisticated and, (possibly interrelatedly) simultaneously more homely and, dare we say it, plebeian. This combination is another factor in their ability to flourish in the long term.

Just as much of what is now regarded as quintessentially Italian or French haute cuisine is largely derived from peasant food, so a good part of what passes for the essential English seaside experience – from paddling in the shallows, a means of avoiding bathing fees, to eating oysters and cockles, then seriously non-U foods – hails from the mores of the Victorian urban lower-middle and working classes. To prolong the culinary theme, fish and chips – a meal never quite better than when sampled off paper and using a slightly ineffectual wooden fork to prong morsels of white fillet and fried spud into the mouth while the pungent aromas of vinegar and caramelised batter mingle with damp briny sea air – is one of the most obvious examples.

The dish was a metropolitan creation. Despite a plausible and near contemporary alternative claim from Oldham in Lancashire, the first fish and chip shop in Britain opened in Bow in 1860. At that time fried fish, introduced to this country by Portuguese Jews in the sixteenth century, was primarily a fodder of the city-dwelling poor. In Charles Dickens's *Oliver Twist*, published in 1838, Fagin ('The Jew') seeks out Bill Sikes in Saffron Hill, a district low enough to possess 'a fried-fish warehouse' and a slew of 'filthy shops' vending pilfered handkerchiefs. Chipped potatoes were a similarly modest fare and hawked in backstreet Irish hot spud shops to needy labourers and their hungry kith and kin. It was, by all accounts, Joseph Malin, an enterprising caterer of possibly either Jewish and/or Cornish extraction, who began to sell parcels of fried fish and chips together from a premises on the Old Ford Road. This winning combination, as if by magic, then suddenly became available from victuallers in every major industrial town and eventually gravitated to the coasts with the trippers in the last years of the nineteenth century.[11] Keen as such visitors were to enjoy the novelty of sea and sand, they also wanted the cheap foods they were (by now) accustomed to – a culinary phenomenon to be played out again some seventy years later when the first English package tourists

---

11 It was the consumption of fish by Londoners that had sustained many of the south coast resorts, when they'd been merely fishing villages. In the days before pleasure seekers arrived, when four out of five residents were engaged in fishing, the bulk of the daily catch from Brighton, for example, had gone up to Billingsgate.

washed up on the beaches of Benidorm and the Costa Del Sol and refused to touch any of that 'foreign muck.' (A position that seems even more ludicrous when we consider the Hiberno-Sephardic-Kernewek origins of their preferred comestible.) So an entire coastal gastronomic tradition, it could be argued, stems from that once widespread English trait, unadventurous eating.[12]

Ice cream, while boasting a more illustrious pedigree, was another comestible that moved from city street to seaside during the same period. In the ages before refrigeration, ice itself was an expensive commodity, one that had to be harvested from the seas around Greenland and Norway and then shipped back to England and stored in brick-lined pits or cooling houses for the summer months. Accordingly, 'iced cream' arose as a delicacy and was originally perfected by chefs to the Italian and French royal courts, in the fifteenth century. Charles II, who sat out the Parliamentary period in France and Holland and was ever a monarch for a rich and fiddly dessert, seems to have brought it to Britain with him at the Restoration. He is recorded as being served it at a feast for the Knights of the Garter at Windsor in 1672. A century later, 'ices' were being dispensed at 'Venetian' Masquerades at Ranelagh Pleasure Gardens in Chelsea. While the confectioner Domenico Negri was offering 'all Sorts of Ice, Fruits, & Creams in the best Italian manner' from a shop 'at the Pineapple in Berkeley Square'.

12 The ubiquity of British grub in Spanish resorts was ruefully noted in one episode of the 1980s-set BBC cop show, *Ashes to Ashes*. DCI Gene Hunt, back from a spell on the Costa Del Crime, informs his colleagues: 'I've been abroad. The Isle of Wight. That was shit. So I went to Torremolinos. Best full English I've ever had.'

By 1779, this firm, now known as Gunter's, were purveyors of confectionary to the royal household, supplying George III and his heirs, the Prince of Wales and the Duke of Clarence (the future William IV) with ices in London, at least. (In an exchange of letters between Jane Austen and her sister Cassandra in September 1804, Austen complains that 'ice' could not be had for love nor money in Weymouth, George III's favourite seaside resort, a detail that suggests that ice cream was hardly a staple of the seaside dessert trolley at that point.) But in the summer of 1850, Carlo Gatti, a Swiss-Italian 'acquainted with the confectionary business', began to sell ices on the streets of Holborn, then a slum area populated by Italian and Irish immigrants. Mayhew, who noted this new phenomenon the following year in his study *London Labour and the London Poor*, reports that on some days there were as many as twenty carts pounding the area to cope with the demand.

Within a decade and a half Gatti had acquired a cafe, four stalls and an ice storage facility at Hungerford Market, near Charing Cross, a music hall, and had fleets of barrow boys flogging 'penny a portion' ices in summer (and hot potatoes and sweet chestnuts in winter) all around London.[13] Such vendors were known as 'hokey pokey' men, a cockney mangling of the hawkers Italian cry, C'e'

13 It was similar seasonal variations in the English diet that first led Walls, once one of the most illustrious names in the field and the pioneer of the vanilla block and spawner of Mr Whippy, into the ice cream business. Until 1922, they were only a sausage manufacturer. As bangers were far more popular in the winter, Thomas Walls, the head of the firm, hit on the idea of maximising production in the slower months by turning part of their plant in Acton over to ice cream in the summer.

un poco, 'try a little', and their ices were dispensed in small reusable emerald green glasses called 'penny licks'. As magical as these *Wizard of Oz*-esque receptacles might sound, they were appallingly, occasionally lethally, unhygienic. Each glass returned was simply dunked in a bucket of usually none-too-clean water, wiped with a cloth (on hot days, quickly a soiled rag) and then refilled for the next customer. The threat of infection from harmful bacteria, including instances of TB, evidently did not deter trade and 'a la Gatti' carts were a fixture on the Sussex and Kent coasts well before the arrival of edible wafers and cones in 1895 made eating an ice cream a substantially less hazardous occupation.

With some city districts now left empty on Bank Holidays (and by the 1890s it was estimated that some 360,000 Londoners were leaving town for the coast or the country over the August holiday) it wasn't uncommon for costermongers to catch the first train down to the seaside, spend the day plying fruit and what have you and then return home with the last of the trippers in the evening.

And one other perhaps overlooked, but vital capital addition to the seaside, as it were, was the Punch and Judy Man. Punch or 'Punchinello ye Italian popet player' was first spied in England at London after the Restoration. Like ice cream, he seems to have sneaked into the country on the coat tails of Charles II. In 1666 an entry from Pepys's diary runs, 'To Polichineli at Charing Crosse, which is much prettier and prettier, and so full of variety that it is extraordinary good entertainment'. But even as late as the 1940s, when Punch was a seasoned veteran of the sands, he continued to remain a much loved city gent. In a section headed 'Punch To-day' in his wartime biography of the puppet, Philip John Stead glosses over the coasts entirely and describes, instead, a pilgrimage to the Isle of Dogs to witness a performance by a Mr Quigley. Quigley, it emerges, is a salt-of-the-earth East Ender, born within five miles of the Bow Bells, and a true street professional, who doesn't let the little matter of rationing and an air raid earlier in the day interfere with a show that revolves around the stealing of sausages and the violent deaths of men in uniforms and babies. Punch's popularity with the London crowds (and elsewhere, obviously) was, though, what had led him to the beaches in the first place. And his colonisation of this realm from the 1860s onwards was so successful that today he is almost solely thought of as a seaside entertainer.

Since Punch was a survivor of sorts from an earlier age of holidays – the gambols around the May Pole at the Strand (or their revival after Puritanism) and the suppressed (in 1855) St Bartholomew's Fayre – it's perhaps not so surprising that he became such a fixture of the beach revels that largely replaced them. And as a relic, or near as damn it, of the 'Merrie England' pageants that thinkers like William Morris yearned for, he could also be safely enjoyed at the seaside by middle-class Victorians seeking comfort in the continuity of traditions in an era when Cecil Sharp was dusting off the Morris Men. Possibly. Or, who knows, perhaps they just found watching puppets of women and children being repeatedly beaten over the head with sticks an improving spectacle, for some reason . . .

If Punch was something of a throwback to fairs gone by for the Victorians, then the Blackpool Tower and the town's Pleasure Beach, the first permanent coastal amusement park, were to embody the new spirit of the carnival at the seaside.

In *The Blackpool Landlady,* John Walton argues that it was absence of scenic grandeur that, in part, led to Blackpool becoming the first really working-class resort. Its cliffs were 'neither high nor picturesque' and the nearby countryside was 'flat and lacked objects of interest for the cultivated visitor and edification. Medieval churches' (along with fossils then another passion of self-improving vacationers) 'were thin on the ground and landmarks of any kind were at a premium.' Its chief attraction was a 'boisterous sea'. The spectacle of its waves coming up to the houses on the front and the spray blowing across the promenade was 'an unalloyed boon in attracting working-class visitors'. The sea, he states, 'was rightly regarded as Blackpool's greatest free show.'

This could, of course, only keep them entertained for so long. And local entrepreneurs, responding to the desire of mill workers to spend some of their hard-earned cash, stepped up to provide much more cheerfully uninhibited diversions than were at that time to be experienced elsewhere.

A near carbon copy of Gustave Eiffel's structure for the Paris Exhibition of 1889, the Tower, standing at over 500 feet and instantly dwarfing the extensive if low-rise boarding houses along Blackpool's so-called Golden Mile[14] was

14 The small scale but high density of its buildings is another indicator of how the town developed rapidly and in response to the demand for cheap lodgings. The contrast between the gigantism of the 'attractions' and the meagreness of the residential quarters mirrored to a large extent the daily environment of the working-class visitors. Assigned poor, back-to-back terraced houses, the average Northern mill hand inhabited cities dominated by monolithic industrial, civic and ecclesiastical architecture.

a beacon to technological progress in much the same vein as Paxton's Crystal Palace had been nearly twenty years earlier. Nevertheless as a gigantic penis of the North, without putting too fine a point on it, it seems a more atavistic addition to the landscape; a kind of longman of the Lancashire coast in steel and pig iron, if you will. Rising up above the site of Dr Cockers's Menagerie and Aquarium in 1894[15] and incorporating a working circus arena at its base, it was certainly a marker of the seriousness with which Blackpool was now taking the whole business of pleasure. And its construction was financed by a cartel of local businessmen led by the town mayor, John Bickerstaffe.

With its origins in a former gypsy encampment, the rest of the Pleasure Beach, meanwhile, looked more avidly across the Atlantic to Coney Island for its inspiration, assembling over time a phalanx of attractions that would number a Moorish pleasure palace, waxwork tableaux, live camels, snake charmers, Indian yogis, Abyssinian gas drinkers, slot machines, switchback rides, a helter-skelter and a giant Ferris wheel. Though the latter was an imitation of one erected in Earls Court in 1895 rather than anything within reach of Ellis Island, Blackpool, with the Irish Sea at its side, would always glance (wild) westward.

Where necessity can be the mother of invention, as the old saying has it, novelty is an often underestimated factor in the actual 'take-up' of new technologies. Electricity, commemorated in a thunder bolt in Blackpool's official crest, was put to some of its earliest public applications at the seaside, supplying for example the power to run such

15 I know. Dr Cockers? You couldn't make it up.

costal amusements as Magnus Volk's dinky and extant seafront railway at Brighton in 1883 and in 1896 its follow-up, his 'Pioneer' marine tram to Rottingdean, a pure Jules Verne contraption that passed through the ocean on stilts. Promoted as a 'Sea Voyage on Wheels' it never quite recovered, despite extensive repairs, from the damage it suffered in a storm on its opening week, a tempest that coincidentally also carried away the old Chain Pier. Though the famed illuminations would have to wait until after the First World War, most of Blackpool's front and each of its three piers was already bathed in electric light by the 1880s. And it was the urge to ferry punters along that lengthy promenade that led to the first electric street tram in England being established there in 1885. From the pleasurable, something practical was born and vice versa; just as such curiosities as the seafront pier magic lantern shows and turn-the-handle kinescopes and Mutoscopes would pave the way for moving pictures, entertainments and the means to fully document the age for posterity.

And on the eve of Victoria's Diamond Jubilee, Esmé Collings, a Brighton-based photographer and former business partner of William Friese Greene, would turn his movie camera on the holidaymakers on the local beaches. The results were exhibited at the Empire Theatre of Varieties in Leicester Square. Like the mosaics splashed with water in ancient myths, his films of 'Boys scrambling for pennies under the West Pier' to this day continue to bring that seaside flickeringly back to life. A time of imperial certainties and industrial might that would be swept aside by the calamities of the First World War, is conjured up at an efficient, sixteen hand-cranked mechanical frames per second, each picture popping out like bullets from a machine gun. The apparent camaraderie depicted on the sands, as the satirical musical *Oh! What a Lovely War* subsequently dramatised with such aplomb, looks now like a rehearsal for shared horrors of life in the trenches.

4
Thoroughly Moderne

*Murder Under the Sun – Agatha Christie and the
Browning Notion – Going Continental on the English
Riviera – Lidos, Swimsuits and Sun Loungers – Coco
Chanel at Morecambe – Bauhaus in Bexhill*

George Orwell once wrote that it was usually in the most blissful circumstances – Sunday afternoons on the sofa, a belly full of roast dinner with a pipe of shag on the go – that the desire to read about murder took hold. Exchange the sofa for a deckchair, the roast for fish and chips, keep the pipe if you like, add the gently percussive slosh of waves and an August sun overhead and Orwell's proposition goes some way to explaining the ongoing popularity of thrillers as beach reads. Like the seaside holiday itself, the crime novel predominantly functions by dishing up reassuringly recognisable situations, stock figures and tropes. The predictable surprise is what is sought, with favourite authors, much as trusted destinations, coming to be relied upon to deliver subtle variations on the same excitements over and over again.

There is, though, a case to be made for the seaside as the birthplace of the English detective novel. It was in between examining nautical malingerers and Senior Service retirees at his medical practice in Southsea that Arthur Conan Doyle wrote 'A Study in Scarlet', the tale that in 1887 bequeathed Sherlock Holmes and Doctor Watson to the world. While nearly a quarter of a century later, in Torquay, a twenty-year-old Agatha Christie, recovering from a bout of influenza and bored of eking out the dreary recuperative hours at home with jigsaws, card games and fashioning small figures from bread dough, tried her hand at writing stories. Inspired by Conan Doyle, she created the Belgian detective Hercule Poirot.[16]

16 An effete moustache-waxer with his dyed hair, astonishingly deductive 'liddle grey cells' and frankly absurd accent, Poirot is the devilishly smart Continental as only the English could conjure. *N'est-ce pas?* He is really as English a

The interwar years are often called the Golden Age of the Detective Story. It was certainly in this period that the form, later immortalised in the game Cluedo and virtually trademarked by Christie, who knocked out seventeen-odd Poirot novels and countless short stories between 1920 and 1939, was at its popular height. Here was the fictional universe where seemingly no dressed-for-dinner house party guest in England was ever free from the risk of cyanide-laced champagne. Nor stately home library floor without its corpse.[17]

But it was also in this same time frame that much of England's landscape and society was irreparably changed. Perhaps one of the most painful truths to emerge out of the cataclysms of the First World War was that the nation had needed America and Canada to win the conflict. Remaining an island, aloof and imperially superior, was no longer an option afterwards. Since that aloofness had, in effect, led to the slaughter of a generation, an urge to embrace outside influences and fresh thinking was that much stronger anyway. New personal moralities and technologies, some of them hothoused during the war, now evolved at a remarkable pace.

confection as a Lyons Swiss Roll or a Mr Kipling Viennese Whirl. The character was partly based on some Belgian wartime refugees in Torquay that Christie befriended while working at a local dispensary.

17 And what was Connie Booth and John Cleese's Torquay-based sitcom *Fawlty Towers* if not a subtle variant on the classic Christie-Cluedo formula? The whole cast – from the hen-pecked but impossible Basil, his wife Sibyl, the blimpish Major Gowan and the dotty spinsters Misses Tibbs and Gatsby to the level-headed Polly, cockney chef Terry and the thickly-accented Spaniard, Manuel – could, at a push, be slotted into *The Mousetrap* virtually unaltered.

The motor car increasingly shrank distances and started to open up the countryside. The layouts of towns, suburbs and cities were reconfigured and along the coasts, commuter dormitories and ribbons of bungalows sprang up. Talking pictures (the most popular ones usually hailing from Hollywood), wireless radio sets and paperback Penguin books sped up the exchange of ideas and information, sowing in turn fresh dreams and aspirations. Women, having coped without men during the conflict and tasted freedoms previously denied them, got the vote and exercised ever-greater liberties, casting off their stays, cutting their hair and raising their hemlines. This rationalisation of dress, coupled with a greater mixing of the sexes socially, also helped to birth an entirely new beach aesthetic.

And it is this, admittedly quite particular, transformation that is caught with such clarity in Agatha Christie's *Evil Under the Sun*, a whodunnit where a bottle of fake tanning lotion enjoys a pivotal role in the plot. Appearing in 1941, though set earlier and on a high-class island retreat off the coast of Devon, it is a surprisingly instructive read on the contemporary customs of the English seaside. While the vision of England that Christie tirelessly dishes up can be so crumbly retrograde as to be practically feudal, (aristos may occasionally be donkeys in her tales but servants and working police stiffs are never lions) she herself liked 'moderne' design and lived in a Welles Coates *machine á habiter* block at Lawn Road in Hampstead during the Second World War. And her books, since they are concerned with the wealthy and pay as much attention, frankly, to the food and furniture as characterisation, often provide compelling glimpses of the nation at its most receptive to the most fashionable of international mores.[18]

As the novel opens, we find Christie's 'plucky' Belgian detective Hercule Poirot lounging about in 'an improved type of deckchair' (no finger-trapping, constantly-collapsing, striped canvas job for him) on the terrace of the Jolly Roger Hotel on Smuggler's Island, Leathercombe Bay. Leathercombe Bay has flourished as a tourist destination, we are informed, ever since '1922' when, according to Christie, 'the great cult of the Seaside for Holidays was finally established and the coast of Devon and Cornwall was no longer thought too hot in the summer.' The Jolly Roger was once the private residence of Captain Roger Angmering, an eighteenth-century sea dog regarded as one mast short of a schooner for building a home on the island in the first place. And Christie's description of this property's metamorphosis from mariner's folly into chic, state of the art leisure complex is perhaps worth quoting at length, since it captures, in microcosm, shifts in fashion reflected in English resorts as a whole.

Throughout the 1920s, Angmering's 'sturdy house', she writes, 'was added to and embellished. A concrete causeway was laid down from the mainland to the island. "Walks" and "Nooks" were cut and devised all round the island. There were two tennis courts, sun-terraces leading down to a little bay embellished with rafts and diving boards . . . And

18 The same contradiction is surely also found in Ian Fleming's James Bond. As a British Imperial warrior he was an anachronism, but with his knowledge of expensive brands and his ability to master a menu in any restaurant in the world, he was the coming man of consumerism.

from June till September (with a short season at Easter) the Jolly Roger Hotel was usually packed to the attics. It was enlarged and improved in 1934 by the addition of a cocktail bar, a bigger dining room and some extra bathrooms. The prices went up.

People said, "Ever been to Leathercombe Bay? Awfully jolly hotel there, on a sort of island. Very comfortable and no trippers or charabancs. Good cooking and all that. You ought to go."

And people did go.'

Concrete causeways, tennis courts, diving boards, sun terraces and cocktail bars: all of this is a far cry from the trusty constitutionals on the sands and high-collared perambulations on the pier of the seaside before the First War, as Poirot himself rather mournfully reflects. Dressed in a white suit and Panama hat, the Belgian is the spit of Thomas Mann's Gustav von Aschenbach and, similarly, sits gazing down upon semi-naked youths on a beach, some of whom are 'lying stretched out in the sun' while others are 'anointing themselves with oil.'

Faced with this array of bronzed and sexually indeterminate figures, ("They are not men and women. There is nothing personal about them. They are just bodies!", the sleuth grouses to his fellow loungers) Poirot begins to extol the virtues of a more modest age now gone. "When I was young, one saw barely the ankle," he states, before coming over all Cole Porter. "The glimpse of a foamy petticoat, how alluring! The gentle swelling of the calf – a knee – a beribboned garter . . ." Before this Proustian jaunt down lingerie lane gets too out of hand, Mrs Brewster, a games mistress type given to making 'gruff comments', fortunately intervenes. '"Much more sensible – the things we wear nowadays"', she observes, with the wisdom of a woman who can remember only too well the full horror of foamy petticoats.

Mrs Gardener, a visiting American, whose husband often has concerns about the 'sanitary arrangements' of English guesthouses, rallies to Mrs Brewster's side.[19] '"Why yes, M. Poirot, I do think, you know, that our girls and boys nowadays lead a much more natural healthy life. They just romp about together and they – well, they – they think nothing of it, if you know what I mean?"'

Poirot, world-weary to a fault, knows exactly what she means. The conversation takes a turn for the surreal at this point, however, as Mrs Gardener starts to expound her pet theory about sunbathing, a practice she believes encourages hair growth.[20] Although sunlight can improve hair growth through stimulating Vitamin D absorption, it is unlikely to lead to hirsute outbreaks of the kind Mrs G imagines. Tanning, though, takes time, and in the early part of the twentieth century it was mainly the rich – the kind of people the well-off Mrs Gardner could share hotel

19 Although normally depicted as fools with too little (Old World) sense and too much (New World) money, the presence of so many Americans in Christie's fictions is a backhanded compliment to the United States's status in the global pecking order.

20 With their wealthy patrons, transient populations and efficient international transport links, seaside resorts are fine places to commit murder, as Poirot is only too aware. And elsewhere in the novel he notes the unique advantages of the seaside town for any potential killer. As it is the custom in England to go to the beach in August, he argues, would-be murderers can simply pose as innocent holiday makers on the coast and are therefore able to stalk their intended victims without looking anywhere near as suspicious as they might elsewhere.

space with – who possessed the appropriate combination of idle hours and access to sunny climes essential to all-over browning.

Much as thinness was once a sign of poverty and plumpness a badge of affluence rather than their opposites today, the tan had previously been disdained as a mark of low social status. Peasants, farmers, fishermen, travelling tinkers and tramps had tans. They worked outdoors, exposed to the elements, and with their hands. In Victorian England with its Empire, 'the White Man's Burden' in Kipling's phrase, paleness was also mixed up with notions of racial and moral superiority. The Dark Continent was full of heathen savages. It was England's duty to ensure their territories stayed in the pink on standard maps. At home (and abroad), delicate complexions were preferred, with parasols and broad hats deployed to keep tone-changing rays at bay. However, industrialisation, in removing workers from the land and placing them inside sunless factories, and the emergence of a strand of evangelical Christianity that saw godliness in physical exercise, meant the tan gradually lost its associations with manual labour. Gentlemen at Lord's, even those as hirsute as W.G. Grace (perhaps the sun helped with that beard growth, after all?) could hardly avoid getting some kind of tan as they played up and played the game. And as tennis, cycling and swimming grew in popularity, the latter rising after Captain Charles Webb successfully crossed the English Channel in 1875, flushed, if not perhaps, fully browned, features slowly became more acceptable.

By the turn of the century, sunlight was being touted

by the medical profession as a possible cure for tuberculosis. Dr Auguste Rollier, an exponent of 'heliotherapy' or sun therapy, opened a TB clinic in the Swiss Alps in 1903. In André Gide's novel *The Immoralist*, published a year earlier, the weak, tubercular scholar Michel is stirred from his torpor by the sight of the 'beautiful, brown sunburned skins' of the peasants in the fields of Ravello. He duly restores himself to health by swimming in a nearby river and then sunbathing on its grassy banks. Sprigs of wild thyme serve as his après sun balm. Gide's novel is representative of a more prevalent trend in literary and artistic circles that can also be spied in the paintings of Paul Gauguin, the writing of Nietzsche (especially *The Gay Science*), and the fictions of D.H. Lawrence and E.M. Forster. In such works, cold, repressive and hypocritical Northern Europe is frequently contrasted with the supposedly more honest, sexually liberated, earthy and spiritual cultures thriving in the sunnier climes of the Mediterranean and further south. The French Riviera, in particular, as a resort favoured by the rich, fashionable and artistic, was pivotal in nudging the suntan into vogue and, consequently, with the aid of Coco Chanel, onto the pages of *Vogue*.

From the late-nineteenth century onwards, the South West of England itself was touted as 'the English Riviera'. When the Great Western Railways began running a 'fast' train from Paddington to Penzance in 1906 it was christened the 'Cornish Riviera Express'. And Google Christie's native Torquay today and a plethora of tourist information sites hail the South Devon town as 'the heart of the English Riviera.'

Such a coinage seems all the more amusing when we consider that back in the 1870s, Cannes in the South of France was widely promoted in England as the 'Mediterranean Cowes'. Queen Victoria, who was to die at Osborne, her Isle of Wight retreat, in 1901 was a frequent visitor to its French counterpart in the winters of the 1880s. Her presence gave the royal seal of approval to the Riviera – and the French Riviera was fundamentally an English invention. A detail that reveals the whole idea of an English Riviera as an imitation of something that originally attempted to recreate a form of the English seaside for English people in Southern France.

Though distinguished, or perhaps more accurately, merely differentiated, by money and class, the Riviera was, in many respects, a kind of elderly great-great-grandfather to more contemporary English pleasuring spots in Europe like Benidorm or Ibiza. And just as the hedonistic excesses of those places eventually looped back into English life, so the Riviera ended up having some profound influences on its own ancestor.

As we have discussed already, when the option to escape the worst of the English weather on the Continent remained open, those with the means and the maladies (TB, gout, or whatever), chose to exercise it. Madeira, Lisbon, Rome, Naples, Pisa, Malta and Malaga were all favoured wintering spots for (normally) aristocratic invalids or at least aristocrats seeking some kind of respite from the cold and damp of the old country. But between the end of the Napoleonic wars and the signing of the Entente Cordiale, the Riviera towns of Nice, Cannes, Menton, Antibes and Monte Carlo grew into the most prominent haunts of Albion's poorly rich or merely fashionably poorly in the cold months.

In 1822 a severe frost at Cannes destroyed most of the orange trees in the surrounding orchards, leaving much of the indigenous population without work. The Reverend Lewis Way, the English minister at the town's Anglican church, persuaded the ex-pat residents to stump up enough money to pay the local unemployed to build a road along the coast. Way's project became what is still known as the Promenade des Anglais – a five-kilometre stretch of seafronting in the vein of Brighton or Eastbourne that has proved especially attractive to rollerbladers in more recent decades.

Like Brighton before it (and both could, technically, be reached from Victoria train station) the Riviera was soon a place where the English upper crust went to let their hair down as much as for their health. In the years of the Belle Époque and immediately after the Great War, it became a byword for exotic self-indulgence. In the popular imagination it was the playground of the world's wealthy, a perpetual marvellous party where the beau monde and demi-monde from across the globe met to exchange witty repartee on the decks of yachts or across gaming tables. Here, or so salacious reports liked to claim, licentiousness was rife, fortunes lost and found, everyone feasted mightily on caviar, and a sea of champagne to rival the Mediterranean was drunk each and every night.

Until the late 1920s, however, the Riviera remained a wintering resort. By 1934 and in *Tender is the Night,* F. Scott Fitzgerald was able to look back on the days when the Riviera was left 'deserted after its English clientele went north in April' with the wry bemusement of a university don pondering stone axes and Cro-Magnon man. But then Fitzgerald, along with his wife Zelda, was part of a fashionable transatlantic sun-worshipping set, centred around the artist Gerald Murphy and his wife Sara, who had succeeded in reversing the seasonal polarity of the resort. The Murphys' own villa – the Villa America – at Cap d'Antibes, visited in the summer months by the likes of Pablo Picasso and Ernest Hemingway, possessed a flat roof that was expressly given over to sunbathing, a novel design feature soon taken up in seaside architecture on both sides of the Atlantic.

Although having to contend with slightly chillier conditions, this cult of the sun inevitably found plenty of disciples in England, as the oiled-bodied littering the terraces of Christie's Jolly Roger Hotel attest. Amusingly, John Fairfield, reviewing *Evil Under the Sun* for the *Spectator*, complained that its weather was too good to be believed, 'a spell of unbroken fine weather outlasting a Poirot investigation on the Cornish coast', he wrote, 'strains the reader's credulity almost to breaking point.' It was Devon, but he had a point.

As with that other more recent import from warmer quarters, the barbeque, the English were not going to let their national climate dissuade them from incorporating Continental-style solar worship into their week in, say, Bournemouth. Not least when Bournemouth was soon aggressively promoting itself as 'A Mediterranean Watering Place on the English Channel' and 'The Centre of Health and Sunshine'.

But from the late 1920s onwards, English resorts increasingly vied for visitors by playing a sunnier than thou game. Holidaymakers were encouraged to 'Travel Sunwards to Hastings and St Leonards', Swanage was 'For Sunshine and Health', Morecambe was on 'The Sunset Coast' while Southern Railways simply labelled all of its dominions 'the Sunny South'.

With this increased fealty to the sun came a corresponding heed of the physical body. And the craze for exercise went hand in hand with the desire, or need, to disrobe to either perfect or show off a tan. Leaner figures heralded by the Flappers, those Bernices with bobbed hair shimmying to the Black Bottom in 1920 and picked out in the serpentine lines of Art Deco's pseudo-Oriental decoration, now tended to be preferred for women. Though, naturally, this shift in feminine shape was not to everyone's tastes. Back again at the Jolly Roger, Major Barry, an ex-army man happiest when reminiscing about 'fakir fellers' in India, complains to Poirot that the 'good-looking fillies' sunning themselves are 'a bit on the thin side' for him.

If *Vogue* magazine is to be believed, though, there initially appears to have been some concern that water sports, far from slimming the body, could have the opposite effect. In 1923 the fashion bible warned its readers that 'swimming' had 'a way of increasing the girth in an amazingly short time.' But swimming, in providing clean and healthy opportunities to frolic in the semi-nude with or without the opposite sex, was embraced, like smoking and applying make-up in public, as a totem of emancipation and equality. In 1926, the American Gertrude Ederle became the first woman to swim the English Channel, beating the men's record by more than two hours. Figure-hugging one-piece costumes such as those produced by Jantzen, who marketed 'The Suit That Changed Bathing into Swimming', far skimpier than earlier outfits, also made uninhibited movement far easier for women. And new fitted rubber bathing caps, sleek and cranial as choco-late Maltesers or embossed with contemporary geometric patterns, meant ducking and diving could be undertaken safe in the knowledge that a newly permanently waved hairstyle would remain intact. While high-waisted trunks for men, fashioned in machine-knitted wool and normally kitted out with a belt and covering the navel, allowed the fellars to show off their athletic prowess without loss of decorum in mixed company.

This being England, keeping up appearances obviously still mattered. But appearing to be more carefree and spon-taneous became a marker of sophistication in the 1920s. Anything else, as Evelyn Waugh's Nina in *Vile Bodies* might say, was simply too tiresome. Where only fifteen years earlier, 'decent' girls had been expected to use a wheeled wooden box to reach the water, they now rolled up, set to go, in brightly coloured beach pyjamas. Worn over a costume, these cotton or crêpe de Chine garments were considered shore-worthy when teamed with a floppy straw hat and heels, but could be slipped off easily if a swim seemed in order.

Men, too, prowled the coasts dressed as if poised for sport, or having temporarily mislaid a recently moored yacht. Hats and ties were abandoned entirely by the young, and open-necked shirts mixed with a jacket or blazer, preferably striped or navy and bearing a club or nautical insignia, and wide-legged cream or grey flannel 'bags' and correspondent shoes. Plus fours, once (if perhaps mystifyingly at this juncture) a practical piece of clothing for golfers – the roll of loose cloth over the knee seemingly encouraging a limber swing on the green – were, thanks to Edward the Prince of Wales, now adopted as dashing seaside wear. The 'Fair Isle', a busily patterned knitted tank top or sweater vest also favoured by the Prince, was another piece of ersatz Celtic kit to be spied on English piers and beaches.

Outward expressions of fitness and leisure, these sartorial affectations pioneered by 'the fast set' were worn, much as miniskirts or flared trousers were in a later period, to show an open-mindedness about pleasure, a thumbing of noses at the stiffer codes and strictures that had predominated before. Accompanying this throwing off of formality in dress was a removal of ceremony in eating out and drinking, with new seaside tearooms, cafes, dance halls and hotel cocktail bars gradually providing less judgmental spaces for the younger men and women to mingle. Full evening wear might still be required for dinner in top hotels. But even an out and out bounder like Ernest Gorse in Patrick Hamilton's *The West Pier* could slip into the 'Oriental palace' of Brighton's Metropole bar to ply his shop girl victim Esther with G and Its by wearing a lounge suit and a purloined Westminster School tie. The waiters were, of course, not fooled but money would speak louder than schooling for the time being.

Quite what did, and did not go, in these oh so modern times could sometimes be confusing. In *Right Ho, Jeeves*,

published in 1934, Bertie Wooster, returning from Cannes
via the highly exclusive Blue Train[21] 'looking bronzed and
fit', is surprised to discover that his latest purchase, 'a
white mess jacket' that was the toast of the Côte d'Azur,
meets with such universal disapproval when donned
on native soil. But the impulse to bring a touch of that
South of France *je ne sais quoi* home was irresistible and,
increasingly, English seaside towns attempted to remodel
themselves architecturally on European lines. This was as
much out of self-interest as anything else. If they hoped to
retain visitors who might, given half the chance, skip over
the Channel or head off on a cruise, they needed to prove
they could cut it with the Continentals, while offering the
ease of the mother tongue and access to garlic-free foods
and drinkable water as a clincher on the deal. Arguably,
their positioning on the edges of the county also made
them, particularly at this juncture, doubly receptive to
what might previously have been felt almost dangerously
cosmopolitan influences.

From the Regency onwards, the fantastical elements of
English seaside architecture had mostly hailed from the
nation's own Imperial realms, with Oriental pagodas and
Indian temples, as we've seen, something of a special-
ity. Though, of course, the high Gothic of many a seafront
Metropole or Grand Hotel usually owed something to
Chartres or Bruges. But in the era of electric light bulbs and

---

21 This trans-European transport of delight, the first train to boast a cocktail
lounge, also provided the setting for one of Christie's fictions, *The Mystery of
the Blue Train*. A corpse-in-an-opulent-compartment forerunner to *Murder on
the Orient Express*, it was a novel that even she had the good grace to describe
as 'easily the worst book I ever wrote'.

the cinema such features, and the stolid redbrick of seaside hotels, started to seem dowdy, provincial and arcanely Victorian. In any case, most of the larger Victorian hotels, some of the finest examples of which do survive to this day, had originally been built to cater for guests with their own servants in tow. And domestics were to be another casualty of the Great War, with only the extremely wealthy hanging on to their staff, though often in reduced numbers. Their facilities, not to say their plumbing, had to be substantially revised to meet the demands of this, quite genuinely, much more streamlined age.

Virtually the entire Victorian period became a pejorative to the Bright Young Things. With even the Tudorbethan oak-beamed world of 'Merrie England' somehow seeming preferable by comparison, at least when combined with a link to the Metropolis by a tube train line or an arterial road. As fun as it was to take time out to pop up and see Nanny Hawkins in the nursery after an afternoon of wine, strawberries and a spin in the open-topped roadster, modern life lay elsewhere.

What was demanded was more functional construction; facilities that, in an age of Bakelite, were hygienic, efficient and free from the extraneous leg-covering-for-tables-type clutter of Victoria and Albert. And while a taste for gaudy exoticism would always be retained in Art Deco – Howard Carter's excavation of Tutankhamun's tomb in 1923 and a further outbreak of Egyptomania fed into the mix – many of the buildings to arrive on the coast in the 20s and 30s paid homage to the sleek, aerodynamic machine-tooled bodies of aeroplanes, electric trains and transatlantic ocean liners.

Blindingly obvious though it might be, the latter was nonetheless the most persistent influence on contemporary English seaside architectural style. Such developments were mocked by Osbert Lancaster in his satirical history of a fictional resort, *Progress At Pelvis Bay* in 1936. 'The keynote of the scheme of decoration adopted', he writes, amusedly, of Pelvis's Ship Hotel, 'was that of a ship, and every effort was made to emphasize this nautical idea in all the details of the furnishing, with such successful results that the illusion of being on ship-board is almost complete and is only slightly impaired by the uninterrupted view of the sea obtainable from most of the windows; were it invisible there would be nothing to indicate that one was not on the most modern of transatlantic liners'.

In the same year that Lancaster's book appeared, one of his fellow contributors to the journal the *Architectural Review*, the artist Paul Nash, had published an article entitled 'Swanage or Seaside Surrealism'. Nash was living in Swanage at the time, and had become convinced that this Dorset seaside town was 'definitely . . . surrealist.' As that old joke about how many surrealists are needed to change a light bulb (answer, 'a fish') amply illustrates, the associating of things aquatic with the curious and bizarre has become something of a cliché of surrealism. (At the London International Surrealist Exhibition at the New Burlington Gallery, also in 1936, Salvador Dali very nearly suffocated giving a lecture clad in a full diving suit and helmet that no one had the foresight to connect to an air supply.) And leaving aside, for the moment, Nash's precise definition of seaside surrealism, it's hard not to feel that at this juncture the seaside was indeed becoming a mite more surreal.

Even today, standing beneath Marine Court in St Leonards – Kenneth Dalgleish and Roger Pullen's fourteen-storey, curved, concrete and steel hymn to Cunard's Queen Mary, completed in 1938 – there's a giddying sense that the time-honoured distinctions between the sea and the land have come unstuck somehow. Like a reverse version of the Crimson Permanent Assurance office block turned pirate ship in Monty Python's *The Meaning of Life*, Marine Court could be a luxury liner that for reasons of its own – seasickness, ichthyophobia, a dislike of pilots – simply decided to forgo the ocean waves and beached itself instead a hundred yards or so further inland.

Perhaps a less sublimely monolithic but no less delightful example of this maritime Deco form is the Burgh Island Hotel at Bigbury on Sea in Devon, the real life model of Christie's Jolly Roger. Though, in the years when it fell into disrepair, (caught or partially anticipated in the 1965 Dave Clark Five big-screen vehicle, *Catch Us If You Can*, where Clark's on-screen girlfriend remarks that it 'smells of dead holidays') it looked more like a wedding cake furiously licked by a mangy dog than a nautical craft as such.

Designed by Mathew Dawson (though further modernised by Paul Roseveare) for Archibald Nettleford, a wealthy industrialist with showbiz connections – he owned the Comedy Theatre in London and the Nettleford Film Studios in Walton-on-Thames – Burgh Island was a gleaming white marvel with a nineteenth-century captain's cabin salvaged from the HMS *Ganges*, incorporated, slightly impishly, into its clean-lined fascia. Reached from the mainland at high tide by a sea tractor, its secluded location made it especially appealing to those in the public eye. Alongside Christie, who also wrote (and set), *And Then There Were None* there (Burgh Island initially appeared in the novel under a pseudonym derived from the book's original, and racist title which I will draw a veil over), it counted Nöel Coward, Louis Mountbatten and the Prince of Wales and Wallis Simpson as guests.

In those halcyon days, Pimms Cup and champagne could be sipped on the water's edge while the house band – the Mayfair Four led by Harry Roy, whose 1931 composition 'My Girl's Pussy' was frightfully naughty if taken the wrong (or the right) way – performed on a diving platform in the centre of the Mermaid Rock Pool. Dogs and children were banned and the hotel was always vigilant in matters of evening dress. It was also known, among those in the know, for its discretion. No questions were ever asked about who arrived (or left) with whom. Which was probably just as well.

Where Burgh Island was exclusive and solely a product of private enterprise, some of the most 'moderne' creations to be erected at the English seaside were conceived with slightly more civic ideals in mind. It is really in the interwar years that local authorities assumed a greater responsibility for the commercial success of their boroughs' amenities. In 1923 the government had enacted legislation that allowed councils more autonomy over spending on public buildings for entertainment. Using ratepayers' money to acquire or lease property and land that remained in private hands, many seaside councils also embarked on ambitious rebuilding plans. During the Depression of the early 30s, schemes such as the extension of Brighton's Marine Drive and the construction of the Undercliff Walk from Black Rock to Rottingdean were undertaken with assistance from the government works programmes – an indigenous update of sort on the Reverend Lewis Way's idea for the Promenade des Anglais on the Riviera. Though, in this instance, the recruitment of unemployed Welsh miners to do much of the work, angered locals.

A chic new modernist swimming pool at Black Rock, the brainchild of the borough engineer David Edwards, that boasted a neon-lit entrance tower, a stylishly curvy cafe and changing rooms and 'one of the cleanest, most durable and most efficient promenade terraces on the South coast' when it opened in 1936, however, was one of the plan's real boons to the area.

The Midland Hotel in Morecambe, replacing a turreted Victorian monster of the same name, was another child of the Depression. Built by the London Midland & Scottish Railway Company in the hope of improving its own stock and revitalising a weary resort in a testing period, its unabashed glamour and modernity speak of a faith in art and progress that seems nothing short of awe inspiring now. An aerodynamic swoop of Snowcreted brick, whose white exterior walls contained crushed fragments of blue glass that twinkled in the sun, the Midland must have looked like a visiting flying saucer, one very probably liberated from the Planet Mongo by a whippy-haired Buster Crabbe, when it opened in 1933.

Standing three storeys high with a flat roof for sunbathing, its convex frontage faced out toward Morecambe Bay, insuring most of its suites and all of the public rooms benefited from a sea view. Its concave, landward side, meanwhile, was dominated by a glorious central double-glazed entrance tower. Housing a gleaming staircase and topped off with a solarium, this was illuminated at night and decorated on the outside with two seahorses by the sculptor Eric Gill.

The hotel was conceived by Oliver Hill, a one-time Arts and Crafts man who'd warmed to modernism after a trip to Sweden in 1930 and who would go on to supply the St Pancras Hotel in London with a swish American Diner. Paying attention to the minutest detail, from designing the curved chairs for the dining room to coming up with seasonal outfits for the chambermaids, Hill harnessed the talents of some of the most extraordinary artists of the age to realise the interior decoration. Along with the seahorses, Gill also produced a bas-relief in Portland stone of 'Odysseus Welcomed from the Sea by Nausicaa' as an emblem of hospitality, and a plaster ceiling medallion inscribed with a line from Wordsworth – 'Oh hear old Triton blow his wreathed horn.' Edward Bawden and Eric Ravilious contributed pictorial frescos and fantastical murals for the children's room and the tearooms. And Marion Dorn designed carpets, rugs and marine motifs that were deployed in the marbled floored mosaics, and on crockery and light fittings.

No expense was spared on the furnishings, with weathered sycamore, white bur and Nigerian cherry used, respectively, for hall chairs, dining-room panelling and bedroom suites. Though obviously setting its stall out for the luxury end of the market, and Coco Chanel would pitch up from Cap d'Antibes in a flying boat that she'd moor in the bay, the hotel was not divorced from the municipal

promenade. Its circular cafe, glazed with lighthouse glass
and decked out with tables of pink Vitrolite, was open to
bathers at the nearby Super Swimming Stadium, the vast
outdoor pool completed in the year of the Berlin Olympic
games.

After the Midland, Hill became involved in an ambitious project to create a new modernist seaside village at
the Frinton Park Estate in Essex. The scheme, sadly, found-
ered after only thirty or so villas were built but he was also
invited to enter a competition to design a new pavilion at
Bexhill-on-Sea, in East Sussex.

Innovation wasn't entirely unknown in Bexhill-on-Sea.
Often trumpeted as the first resort in Britain to publicly
sanction mixed bathing, in 1895, (though this claim is
largely discounted nowadays) it had hosted one of the earliest international cycling tournaments two years later and
was quick off the mark when it came to moving pictures;
The Kursaal, the town's original entertainment pavilion,
starting to show films back in 1898. And in 1902, Bexhill
seafront became the very first place in Britain to host motor
racing. The largest landowner in the area, the 8th Earl
De La Warr, the chairman of the Dunlop Tyre Company,
importing the idea from Nice, where the previous winter
he'd seen the debut of world motor rallying. But Bexhill
was better known for what it didn't do – or allow – than
what it did. The tawdrier entertainments common to most
seafronts – minstrels, hawkers, you name it – were banned
in Bexhill and their absence was a matter of local pride.
Brighton could keep its dog and horse tracks and Hastings
its Pierrots and pier. Somehow even distinguishing itself
from respectable old Eastbourne up the road, Bexhill was

a place favoured by the kind of well-heeled sojourner or pensioner who was genuinely looking for a quiet, if reasonably distinguished, spell by the sea. In 1907, the quite reasonable suggestion that a Winter Garden might please all-year-round visitors met fierce opposition. The compromise, a Colonnade Bandstand, was hard fought and still attracted accusations that that place was in danger of becoming too 'trippery'.

Until 1913, when a dispute between the Earl and the municipality over the going rate for the land was finally resolved and the council acquired ownership, the seafront had remained partitioned for almost eighteen years. In the aftermath of the Great War, though, when many of its most affluent seasoners had abandoned it for Cannes or Biarritz, the need to attract fresh visitors and residents became much more pressing. Initially, however, this was resolved by an influx of wrinklies as the region, banding together under the tourist banner 'the Conqueror's Coast', grew into a popular retirement belt. While Southern Railways began to electrify their network – their Brighton Belle express was a kind of short-stop *le train bleu* – making the Sussex coast a far more attractive proposition to a growing band of commuters by the early 1930s.

Despite all this, or possibly because of it, there was a sense that Bexhill needed to do something else if it was to thrive, or, arguably, survive. Why, even neighbouring Hastings and St Leonards, under the leadership of a new borough engineer, Sidney Little, had ripped up its trams, then a decidedly lower-class means of transport, and refashioned its promenade into an impressive twin-decked, concrete walkway. Clean new shelters, futuristic modular pods, were to spring up along it. In another forward thinking move an underground car park was landscaped into the front with the aim of keeping unsightly traffic away from the beach. While the White Rock Pavilion Theatre, designed in a colonial-style but executed in modern materials by Charles Cowles-Voysey in 1927 and costing over £100,000, represented the acme of entertainment venues. And for those who found the sea, with its fish, rocks, weeds, salt and god knows what else, a little passé, there was by 1933 an enormous new outdoor swimming pool to bathe in.

Here, alas, hubris seems to have got the better of everyone. At over 330 feet in length, and with three promenades, one walled with sun-trapping Vita glass, terraces to accommodate 2,000 seated spectators, a cafe and two sunbathing decks, this reinforced concrete structure, an amphitheatre faced with tinted cement, was nearly twice the size of the later pool at Black Rock, and ultimately, simply too big for the town's needs.

Still, all this could only give little Bexhill pause for thought. But it wasn't until the town elected a vigorous young new mayor in 1932 that plans for a new music venue, long ruminated upon, finally got underway. Edward Dundonald Brassey Sackville was the 9th Earl De La Warr, his father and grandfather had to all intents and purposes built the town. As the first hereditary peer to represent the newly formed Labour Party in the House of Lords and as the man who would go on to lay the foundations for the Festival of Britain, the national telephone system and independent television, 'Buck' De La Warr was a genuinely radical politician. A socialist and friend of Nancy Cunard, he fervently believed that art and innovative contemporary design could only improve the lot of ordinary lives. With Hitler now denouncing the modernist architecture that Walter Gropius and the Bauhaus school had pioneered in Germany as 'Bolshevik' and decadent, the style took on an additional moral force for the Left in Britain: to be pro modern architecture was also to be anti-Fascist. And with black-shirt rallies being held along the Sussex coast in Bognor Regis and Worthing and the latter town subsequently electing a fascist councillor in 1934, these issues, which might seem rather unrelated to the cut and jib of a new seaside concert hall, were far more potent then.

De La Warr was convinced that Bexhill not only needed a new pavilion, it needed a pavilion that was newness exemplified. After much personal and legal wrangling, a scheme for the venture was agreed. Its £80,000 costs would, ultimately, be met by local ratepayers who would in return receive discounted tickets for concerts, but a loan from the Ministry of Health was arranged to cover its construction. Only too conscious of the antipathy many of the town's senior citizens felt towards anything invented after 1903, the Mayor arranged that the final design be decided by a competition. But as De La Warr's courting of Oliver Hill and adverts that were placed in the architectural press make plain, there was little doubt about what kind of design was preferred. 'No restrictions as to the style of architecture will be imposed, but', the advert ran 'buildings must be simple, light in appearance and attractive, suitable for a holiday resort.' Heavy stonework was 'not desirable' but 'modern steel-framed or Ferro-cement construction' could be adopted, if they liked. And the winners, Erich Mendelsohn and Serge Chermayeff were not averse to a bit of modern steel-framing or Ferro-cement.

Mendelsohn had only recently arrived in the UK, having fled Germany following Hitler's appointment as chancellor in 1933. Regarded as one of the most outstanding modernist architects in Europe, he had begun his career as a theatrical costume and set designer and had been heavily influenced by the expressionist movement. Marked by their innovative use of glass, concrete and steel, streamlined features, and decorative lettering, his buildings in Germany, particularly for the Schocken department store chain, were dynamic and shapely and forged with a devotion to line and form. Chermayeff was born in Grozny and schooled in England, but had been left an exile after his family's fortune was lost in the Russian Revolution. Variously an illustrator for the Amalgamated Press, a professional dancer – he won an International Tango Contest in 1927 – a cattle rancher and an interior designer for Waring and Gillow, he'd set up his own design practice in 1931. Working on the interiors for the BBC's Broadcasting House with Welles Coates, among others, he'd also produced some arresting radio cabinets for Ecko. And the supple lines of the De La Warr do have the tactile quality of a radio cabinet of that era. But the large plate windows, balconies and its steely staircase all give the De La Warr an almost eerie lightness. It looks like what I imagine the skate-y bit of an ice rink might look like if it could somehow be turned inside out. Its rounded, light form, appropriately given Mendelsohn's own time with Schocken, has long been appropriated for shopping centres and malls, but it still remains convincingly modern. Perched as it is above the domes and balustrades of the earlier Edwardian neo-classical colonnade, it does a good impression of something H.G. Wells might have conjured up back in the day.

When it opened in December 1935 the De La Warr could offer visitors flat roofs for sunbathing, a library, a ground-floor restaurant, lecture halls, and a main auditorium for plays and recitals that doubled as a dance hall. Furniture was by Alvar Aalto and the restaurant mural by Edward Wadsworth, the Vorticist turned 'seaside surrealist'. At the laying of the foundation stone, De La Warr gave a passionate speech in which he proclaimed that the Pavilion would lead to a whole new industry, 'an industry of giving that relaxation, that pleasure, that culture, which hitherto the gloom and dreariness of British resorts have driven our fellow countrymen to seek in foreign lands.'

As an arts and entertainment centre, the Pavilion was not an unqualified success in the 1930s let alone afterwards but facets of Mendelsohn and Chermayeff's design were immediately emulated at other seaside resorts, most obviously at Saltdean near Brighton, where a Lido in a strikingly similar circular style was built in the year the De La Warr opened. But also in Blackpool, where Joseph Emberton had been charged with bringing 'some order into the chaos' of the Pleasure Beach. The corkscrew-headed, discus-like Casino building opened in 1939.

But by then the world, alas has other, more pressing concerns. The rising sun, a symbol deployed on bathing hats and beach towels through the 20s and 30s, would soon enough acquire other associations. Just as many of England's seaside hotels and pavilions would gain fresh employment as barracks and billeting houses.

5
Camp It Up

The Boarding House Blues – Life Under Canvas at
Cunningham's – Coney Island Comes to Skegness
– Billy Butlin, the Beveridge of Leisure

The Holiday Camp enjoys a somewhat ambiguous, uneasy even, relationship with the seaside. In the English collective consciousness it is as much a part of the fabric of the coastal resort as amusement arcades, B&Bs and ice cream parlours. But, while not quite as remote as those airports favoured by budget carriers to major European cities, holiday camps have always tended to keep a certain geographical distance from the main business of the beach. Historically a whippersnapper, this was as much due to issues of availability of land and economy than anything else. And yet, there was, and remains, a deeper estrangement at the heart of the relationship. One that rather naturally stems from the central premise of the holiday camp, at least in its commonly known incarnation.

Rather like a disapproving child to an errant parent, the holiday camp came into existence largely as an admonishment to the mature seaside resort. Where the seaside boarding house landlady would be intractable about the comings and goings of guests, and fond of surcharges, the holiday camp would seek to be accommodating and scrupulously accountable. Where the English weather could only be relied upon to be unreliable, leaving sodden visitors at the mercy of the elements, overpriced teashops and penny-eating slot machines, the holiday camp strove to provide diversions at all hours and in all conditions. In an era when few hoteliers welcomed children and fewer still laid on any facilities for them, the holiday camp revolved around their needs – and understood that parents needed to be free from their brats now and then to fully unwind.

The firm Pontin's once advertised their holiday camps as 'resorts in themselves'. And the holiday camp was, in effect, a way of going to the seaside without having to bother with going to the seaside per se. It might be by the sea – and Butlins for a time billed themselves as 'Butlins by the sea' but practically everything was geared up to make tawdry rock shops and the sludgy grey mass of wavering brine in the near-distance appear the least exciting option. One of the things that consistently irked commentators was the idea that some guests, provided with a steady flow of food, urn-stewed nut-brown tea, keg beer, a chalet, a swimming pool and a jamboree of games, club turns and knobbly knee contests, were happy not to leave the confines of the camp for the duration of their stay. Akin to getting no further than the gift shop or cafe in a museum, such campers were judged to be somehow culturally deficient. Arguably though, they were simply at the forefront of what it was to live in an increasingly consumerist society. A society where leisure and material goods would be available to a far greater percentage of the population than ever before. At its height in the post-Second World War decades the holiday camp represented so much of what it was to be modern in Britain. Like instant coffee, frozen orange juice and drip-dry shirts, this was the old seaside holiday but better. Newer. Brighter. Shinier. It was certainly a lot less Dickensian than a week's half board in the Seaview where armchairs would be covered with antimacassars and doors bolted at the chimes of a grandfather clock in the hall. And you might get to see Cliff Richard or The Bachelors playing in the on-site Pig and Whistle Bar.

This moment is caught almost perfectly in Tony Richardson's big-screen adaptation of John Osborne's *The Entertainer*, a play that tied the fast-fading glories of the music hall to Britain's greater loss of prestige after Suez. Filmed in 1960 and in Morecambe, the resort comes, by implication at least, to feel as much of a relic on borrowed time as the pitiable Archie Rice, played with such bitter wisdom by Laurence Olivier. Just as this third-rate song and gag merchant is dismissed as worthless by one passing punter for never having been 'on the telly', so the all-mod-cons Middleton Towers Pontin's, patronised in the film by Thora Hird in full grasping battleaxe mode, appears as a contemporary town planner's vision of what could be achieved in the old town up the road with a new shopping centre, a car park and a few tons of concrete.

In the year the film was released, Billy Butlin was opening a new camp at Bognor on the Sussex coast. Exemplifying the mood of this go-getting period, one correspondent to the *Bognor Regis Post* that September argued that the arrival of Butlins should mark the start of a much more radical reshaping of the town.

> Tall, modern buildings in the style of Basil Spence, Corbusier or the many other gifted architects practising today are what we hope to see. Nothing pseudo, nothing shoddy. We must not tolerate drab brick boxes. This is our chance to have beautiful architecture reflecting our day and age, and we must seize it with both hands. Fine hotels, luxury flats, solarium, shops, theatres and conference halls, and civic buildings can and should arise, fronted by a broad, impressive seaway.

The fashion for high-rise and concrete would fade. Corbusian machines for living in would soon become more readily associated with sink estates and urban decay than swish beachfront developments, despite the best efforts of such ugly behemoths as Southend's Esplanade Court or Worthing's Grafton and Guildbourne Centre. And it is interesting to note that the social standing of both the concrete block and the holiday camp in England, already dented by the late 1960s, declined sharply and practically in unison in the middle 1970s. In their own ways, each came to seem like slightly embarrassing relics of a more optimistic, if perhaps, faintly coercively conformist age. Even those who have never ventured inside a holiday camp can probably conjure up an image of a Redcoat and some notion of rigorously enforced jollity at the mention of Billy Butlin's name. It demonstrates how successful Butlin's formula was. But it also confirms the dangers of becoming so closely shackled to a specific package in the minds of the public. A shackling that countless changes in ownership, numerous renamings and rebrandings, forays into Continental ventures and luxury boutique hotels have done little to dislodge. Though after all these years it could just start to make some kind of glorious sense again, like the TV talent contest or ballroom dancing, maybe.

Billy Butlin opened his first camp at Mablethorpe near Skegness in 1936. As he readily admitted, he did not invent the holiday camp. Nor were the ones he established quite as unique or revolutionary as the entrepreneur, in his more egotistical moments, liked to maintain. There is, however, no disputing that the scale and ambition of his operation transformed the holiday camp – and holidaying – in Britain and, by extension, life in English seaside towns.

Though he spoke with the gentlest of West Country burrs, Butlin was born in Cape Town, South Africa, a detail that tickled those who felt that there was always a slight whiff of internment about his fenced and gated complexes; the British, after all, having pioneered the concentration camp in the Anglo-Boer War. The product of an ill-starred marriage between the scion of a well-to-do Rugby banking clan and the daughter of a baker turned country showman, Butlin spent a good part of his formative years in Canada. Lying about his age to enlist, he'd served in the Canadian Army during the First World War, acting as a stretcher-bearer at Vimy Ridge, Ypres and Arras. Returning to Toronto after the war, he worked for Eaton's department store before sailing for Britain on a cattle ship. He arrived in Liverpool on 17 February 1921 with, as he often chose to remind people, five pounds to his name, and headed to Bristol to join relatives in the fairground game.

Although he largely dismissed earlier holiday camps in Britain as 'primitive' affairs in comparison with his own, they were the product of the same sort of colonial cross-currents as Butlin himself. Centuries of Imperial adventuring. Muscular Christian evangelical missions to Africa. Large-scale emigration to North America. And the odd, high-Romantic vision of tinkers' wagons and gypsies cocking a snook at the stresses of steam-age life. All of these things had succeeded in imbuing camping, previously an unpleasant necessity in the fields of trapping, exploration and soldiering, with a certain nobility in England by the end of the nineteenth century. Popularised by Thomas Hiram Holding, the author of *The Camper's Handbook* (1908) and a London tailor who as a small boy in the 1850s had crossed the prairies of America as part of a wagon train, its most fervent devotees tended to be on the cranky side:

well-meaning do-gooders, evangelical teetotallers, agrarian socialists, patriotic militarists, pacifistic coreligionists, vegetarians, folklorists, twig-binders and cyclists. But it was the notion that camping could be 'improving' that also led many to pitch their tents beside the sea. Here a sense of adventure and the health-giving salt air could be imbibed along with the damp canvas, unwashed socks, bonfire smoke and whatever physical, spiritual or ideological regime was being pursued. Recruits to Baden-Powell's very first Scout camp in 1907, did their duty on saline-lashed Brownsea Island in Poole Harbour.

And it was at a church Boys' Club, an organisation that was an almost direct precursor to the Scouts, that the beginnings of what most regard as the first 'real' seaside holiday camp in Britain are also to be found. By the time Butlins Skegness opened, Cunningham's International Young Men's Holiday Camp at Douglas on the Isle of Man had been running for over forty years. As the name suggests, there was a distinct gender bias around access to its rows of candlelit bell tents, grand dining room, concert hall, palm house, billiard room, tennis courts, barbers, bank and ninety-foot heated swimming pool. Although by the 1920s women were permitted to attend social functions, they were never admitted as residents. The other rule that remained right until the site's sale in 1945 was a ban on alcohol – a factor that led to the camp possessing one of the first American-style soda fountain bars in the UK. Its founders, Joseph and Elizabeth Cunningham, were avid temperance campaigners who rather more bafflingly also regarded the poetry of Robert Burns to be injurious to morals. Movers and shakers on Liverpool's Christian philanthropic scene, they'd started to arrange seaside summer camps for Toxteth's needy adolescent boys at Llandudno and then at Laxey on the Isle of Man. For lads who scarcely left the squalor of the TB-ridden inner-city tenements, the latter provided the added thrill of a sea voyage.

After falling out with the local institute who helped finance these jaunts, the Cunninghams set about establishing a permanent base on the island and turning the scheme into a business. Drawing on a network of associates in the temperance leagues and Sunday School movement in the region but now freed from an affiliation with any particular denomination, by the turn of the century they were able to attract enough bookings to open their camp from May until October.

Their original philanthropic venture had been rather heavy on self-reliance with guy rope inspections and mess hall duties an intrinsic component of the *mis en scène*. The new camp, however, was purposely more relaxed and strove to shake off any lingering overtones of charity. It still aimed to provide a cheap seaside holiday for single men who might not otherwise be able to afford one but the Cunninghams needed to lure slightly more affluent campers to survive financially. Accordingly, their new camp was operated like a hotel, albeit a hotel where sleeping under canvas, four to a tent, and cold baths were the rule. This situation continued long after it acquired a larger site and a fleet of fine auxiliary buildings, including a miniature castle that housed the washroom and latrines. (To an extent this contrast persisted at Butlins, where campers left grand, potted palm-stuffed ballrooms to return to rather basic chalets.) From now on guests were no longer expected to muck in with cooking and cleaning, and were instead waited upon and encouraged to avail themselves of a wide-ranging programme of sporting events, sing-songs, Sunday concerts and excursions. Or simply kick back with a book from the library on the beach, as one contented visitor explained to *The Tourist* magazine in 1899. 'Far from the maddening crowd, the reader may enjoy his book in perfect peace, while the sea breezes bear to him such stores of ozone as shall fit him for another year of vigorous toil.'

Back numbers of *Cunningham's Camp Herald,* their annual brochure, and numerous period photographs of chaps with luxuriant moustaches and short, neatly parted hair, posing arm-in-arm outside tents, conjure up a vanished world of seemingly uncompromised masculine camaraderie. A world that Sigmund Freud, the Somme and, later, Village People would all play havoc with. Staring at an illustration of a leotard-wearing Strong Man with a dumbbell on the cover of one issue, all bulging biceps and cheery inviting grin, 'camp' seems the only word for it.

What one correspondent for the *Manchester Daily Dispatch* judged, quite in earnest, as 'a brief snatch of Paradise with manly life and manly ways' was more unusual in its day for the mix of men it attracted rather than any insistence on male exclusivity. Sons of Members of Parliament, county councillors and nephews of London physicians billeted with city clerks and shop assistants in a manner that remained extremely rare on Civvy Street before the First World War. The conflict, of course, forcibly brought the classes into intimate contact with one another as never before. Afterwards some veterans would seek to re-establish bonds of comradeship found in the trenches at camps like Cunningham's, itself used to intern enemy aliens during the war.

Although never wavering from its men only guests and booze-free regime, the camp did modernise to meet the desires of an emerging generation who were perhaps more Brideshead than Baden-Powell. A cinema was installed, dances to which women were invited, held, and finally even some of the tents were replaced with wooden huts. The camp chant, a mostly rhetorical, 'Are we downhearted?', however, lasted until the world was at war again.

As a young man in Canada, Butlin had attended a summer camp not unlike those first hosted by the Cunninghams. Held on the shores of Lake Ontario, it had been run by his department store employers in the spirit of benign paternalism common among large companies then. Although no great fan of life under canvas, he'd enjoyed swimming, canoeing and fishing there. But more importantly, Butlin was impressed by the atmosphere, which he summed up as 'happy and friendly, largely due to the fact that everyone paid the same for their holiday and there was no snobbery.' Staying on Barry Island in Wales in the 1920s and lodging at a seaside guesthouse for the very first time, he'd been shocked to find the complete absence of any similar 'atmosphere'. Astounded by the way the guests were treated, in particular that they had to leave the premises after each meal, even if it was tipping down with rain – and it 'rained incessantly all the time', – he, apparently, vowed there and then to set up a holidaying business of his own. Though it would have to wait a decade until he'd built up an empire of eight seaside amusement parks

In the interim period, new holiday camps of various stripes continued to be built in Britain. Some, like those established at Croyde in North Devon by the National and Local Government Officers Association or at Corton near Lowestoft by W.J. Brown, the head of the Civil Service Clerical Association and, subsequently, an MP and frequent panellist on BBC TV's *In the News*, were formed by trade unions, cooperative or mutual societies to provide afford-able retreats for their members.

Brown's Civil Service Camp, which opened in the spring of 1924, was one of the most sophisticated, featuring wooden chalets with running water and electric light, a recreation hall for dancing and concerts, tennis courts, bowling and putting greens, a dark room for photographers along with a baby patrol service for parents, and go-karts and a play-room for the kids themselves.

Brown, like Butlin, had also spent time at a summer camp as a youth. Enduring a bleak week of terrible weather and poor food in a bell-tent at the formerly socialist outfit at Caister in Norfolk left him with a distinct aversion to rough-ing it under canvas. But as the father of three young children, he'd equally found seaside boarding houses a trial. If his offspring were noisy, they upset the other guests and if they tried to be quiet, they soon became sullen and miserable for being unnaturally constrained. And then there was the usual business of being slung out of the place for most of the day on days when it was wet. His camp, like Butlins' much later and larger efforts, was intended to provide government pen-pushers with an antidote to the traditional coastal accom-modation. And it proved popular enough that a second camp was opened on Hayling Island in 1930.

In the private sector, too, there emerged several 'personality' proprietors offering the kind of eye-catching all-in deals that Butlin would soon enough make his own. There was H.E. Potter, or 'Pa' Potter, as he preferred to be known. An avuncular figure, Potter liked to present himself as a sort of Old King Cole of his beach camp at Hopton, Great Yarmouth. By 1933, this facility was already advertising itself as 'THE LUXURY CAMP WITH MODERATE CHARGES AND A FINE CAMP SPIRIT' and boasting of 'BRICK CHALETS with running water' and 'a New BRICK Sun-lounge with claygate fire-place, lavishly furnished with expensive Carpets and 40 modern easy Chairs.' Around the same time and on Hayling Island, 'Captain' Harry Warner, a retired Royal Artillery officer, was presiding over the first of what would become fourteen camps to bear his name. The firm he founded lingers in the hospitality trade to this day. But Butlin ended up overshadowing them all, with the scale of his operation and by introducing a generous sprinkling of razzamatazz to the game.

The timing of his entry into the field is also extremely significant. Rather like reading a book with inky fingers, our awareness of the Second World War inevitably tends to blacken almost everything that precedes it. But an often-overlooked facet of the case for appeasement was that Britain was doing pretty well. Having weathered the worst ravages of the Great Depression, by the late 1930s unemployment was falling, and working weeks were shortening. In the year before the Holiday With Pay Act came on the statue book in 1938, by which point Butlin was cutting the tape on a second camp at Clacton, nearly 15 million Britons were estimated to be spending a week or more away from home each year.

The country, just before the war, was undergoing a real consumer boom with house building and the manufacturing of new domestic goods (radio sets, washing machines and vacuum cleaners etc.) the major areas of growth. Although not published until 1947, Julian Maclaren-Ross's novel *Of Love and Hunger*, a semi-autobiographical tale of Hoover peddling in Bognor, offers an authentic enough glimpse of this era and depicts life in a humdrum seaside town poised between a present of nights at 'the flicks', plate-glass-and-chromium-windowed shops, ersatz coffee and new labour-saving devices and a coming war of blackout curtains and powdered eggs.

The latter, however, appeared a very distant prospect when Freda Monk from Nottingham became the first visitor to Butlins Skegness. Rocking up a day early on 10 April 1936, her eagerness proved something of a consolation in that opening week. At least one large party failed to show, having journeyed to Sheerness by mistake. Or so Butlin, who buffed this tale to perfection in the following decades, always claimed. Whether this story was true or not, Butlin's need to relate it is revealing. Lurking in here, surely, is the suggestion that before he pitched up in town, no bugger had ever heard of Skegness. A suggestion, that perhaps annoyingly, isn't without a certain grain of truth to it.

Arguably, Skegness was quite an unprepossessing place to locate what was then billed as a 'Luxury Holiday Camp.' Though it had initially been developed as a resort back in the 1870s by the Earl of Scarborough, when Butlin first visited Skegness in 1927, there was 'little more than two streets and a short promenade called the Grand Parade'. The whole town, as he recalled, was 'so small you could stand outside the station and see cows grazing in the fields.' Its beaches were (and are) long, and gifted with the kind of yellow sand that on a sunny day puts one in mind of ice cream from the era when Tartrazine still had a free run on the freezer cabinet. But it lies on the Lincolnshire coast, a landscape distinguished by its flatness and, to a degree, the absence of other distinguishing features. As such it is exposed to the North Sea, in all its choppy glory. That the slogan 'Skegness is so bracing' was used on posters to promote the place by the Great North Railway in 1908 is a somewhat telling detail. Although the designer, John Hassela, who devised the slogan and the accompanying image of a fat jolly fisherman cutting a caper, had never set foot in Skegness. And in an epoch of stiff upper lips, cold baths and Newbolt's 'Play up! Play up! And play the game!', the word 'bracing' possessed virtues that decades of inside loos and central heating have made less discernible, desirable even. Herne Bay in Kent, for example, was pronounced 'one of the healthiest places in the kingdom' by the Registrar General in the 1902 edition of *Seaside Watering Places* because it was 'unequalled' for its 'bracing air.'

Ironically, perhaps, given the corresponding loss of ozone quality and rail passenger numbers, it was the arrival of motor charabancs carrying trippers on beanos from the outlying East Midland towns that started to buoy Skegness's fortunes. Butlin, touring some of the old seasonal regional fairs with his hoopla stalls, had begun to notice that punters were slowly ebbing away as the 1920s progressed. Motor coaches, cheaply hired for group and factory outings, were encouraging larger numbers of the urban poor to abandon their traditional pleasuring grounds and take days by the sea instead. Butlin resolved to follow them. In the bar at London Olympia, he received a tip-off about Skegness from a fellow stallholder, and went on to acquire the lease on a stretch of beachfront known locally as 'the Jungle' and set about building an amusement park there. It thrived, helping to put 'Skeggy' on the map and parks at Bognor, Clacton, Felixstowe and Rhyl would duly follow.

In the autumn of 1933, the novelist J.B. Priestley, travelling around the country gathering the material for what would become *English Journey*, had pitched up in Blackpool. Having only caught glimpses of the resort since the Great War, Priestley was perturbed by what he found. To him, the place seemed to lack 'something of its old genuine gaiety'. The Pierrots and the minstrels, once among its chief attractions, had mostly been replaced by 'gangs of carefully drilled young men and women (with nasal accents) employed by the music publishers to "plug" their "Hot Broadway Hits."' The amusements were 'becoming too mechanised and Americanised' and everything had 'developed a pitiful sophistication – machine-made and not really English – that [was] much worse than the old hearty vulgarity.' Whether Priestley would have ever seriously liked the 'old hearty vulgarity' is a moot point. And why American singing should be so much more offensive, or un-English, than French clowns or black-faced turns is trickier to unpick. But Priestley experienced this change as a loss. Possibly much like holiday camps to us today, in their decline the old amusements had accrued a nostalgic value for him. A value that, faced with them a decade or so earlier, he may not have felt.

As the man who brought the first Coney Island dodgem cars to the English seaside, and to Skegness on the Whitsun weekend of 1928, Butlin stood for everything Priestley considered so malign. The creeping Americanisation of English speech, habits and pleasures, in particular, appalled the writer. Woolworths, the Yank dime store chain then jazzing up the nation's high streets, was another bugbear for Priestley and many of his generation. From this distance, and with his holiday camps arc welded into the English imagination, it is perhaps hard to picture Butlin as a figure heralding the arrival of Pax Americana. But conceived along Ford's Model T mass-production lines, his amusement parks and camps were the pinnacle of a transatlantic corporatisation of leisure. That he kitted out all his fairground staff in matching, pocketless, monogrammed jackets, an early exercise in branding and a neat means of stopping them from filching the odd tuppence into the bargain, was itself seen as a novel innovation. Such homogenising trade gimmicks were far more common in the US than here.

As a newspaper profile published around the time that Priestley was packing his bags for Blackpool makes plain, Butlin was viewed as an entrepreneurial new broom in Britain. Headed 'Big Business has come into the English fair world in the person of Billy Butlin', the piece is written in the kind of endlessly upbeat tone you associate with cinema newsreels from the period. Its concluding paragraph chirruped, 'Big business, is modernising the fair, erasing the curious traditions of the fairground which have been handed down from past centuries. The cry "Boys – are you sports?" will soon be a dim echo in the fairgrounds of England, and William E. Butlin, the spirit of common sense, fair play and the value of money, will soar on to ever greater heights of glory, building as he goes another monument to the imperishable saga of British enterprise.'

But business acumen aside, Butlin, who for much of his life sported a thin, matinee idol moustache, recognised that the British public, exposed to Hollywood talkies, Broadway tunes, magazines and advertising, were in awe of the kind of sleek glamour emanating from across the pond. And in the late 1930s, his camps, with their chandelier-lit ballrooms and themed lounges, had the escapist flash of a contemporary Odeon picture palace or an ocean liner. The curtains in the chalets were decorated with nautical motifs, a detail possibly intended to engender the sense of being on a cruise. This idea was certainly picked up by Graham Greene who in 1939 supplied one of the earliest literary sketches of a Butlin-style camp in his novel *The Confidential Agent*. D, the agent of the title, is the somewhat unwilling guest of The Lido, a hotel two miles out of a fictional resort called Southcrawl that is 'more like a village' and is composed of 'circle after circle of chromium bungalows around a central illuminated tower – fields and more bungalows'. As his host, Mr Forbes, explains, it is 'a new idea in popular hotels. A thousand rooms, playing fields, swimming pools . . . we're advertising it as cruise on land. Organised games with a secretary. Concerts. A gymnasium. Young people encouraged – no reception clerk looking down his nose at the new Woolworth ring. Best of all, of course, no seasickness. And cheap.'

Butlin himself was most definitely cheap. Happily confessing to rummaging through the bins to see which items of the menu were going to waste, paying staff what he could get away with, monitoring every pound, shilling and pence spent in his name, he eventually fled to Jersey in the 1960s to escape the punitive taxes of Wilson's government. After the war he bought up army surplus materials, creating bar stools out of bomb casings and using old fighter pilot seats as poolside sun loungers. A bulk purchase of dead stock parachute silk was refashioned and sold as Butlin sun tops. During rationing, whale meat was put into steak and kidney pies or served up heavily garnished with onions and gravy and listed as 'Canadian wind-dried steak'.

There was always a touch of the Wizard of Oz about Butlin's actions. Like the man behind the curtain pulling the leavers or a screen set designer creating the illusion of opulence, carefully arranged sprigs of foliage, marine knick-knacks and the odd glitter ball often did wonders to lend a touch of razzle-dazzle while covering a multitude of interior decor sins. With a nod to the extant architectural style of 1930s suburbia, the des res's millions dreamed of owning, the camp accommodation was initially advertised as 'Cosy Elizabethan Chalets'. Built by Butlin's fairground workers in the off-season months, they were knocked up with timber and chicken wire coated in cement. Nevertheless, painted in candy colours and fitted with electric lighting, carpets and running water, the results often appeared far more homely than some of the guests' own homes.

In these formative years Butlin was similarly creative with his entertainments programme. Discovering that many of the top names spent their Sundays either resting or travelling between dates, since the theatres were dark, he brokered a deal to secure special appearances at the camps at cut-down rates. Will Hay and Elsie and Doris Waters were among the stars of the day happy enough to earn some easy extra cash. A pioneer in harnessing the power of celebrity, he lured the batsman Len Hutton to Skegness the day after his historic 364 runs against Australia at the Oval in 1938. Paying him £100 for a couple of hours, he persuaded the cricketer to stand on the camp's stage with a bat made out of Skegness rock and face down balls from the comedienne Gracie Fields. Some five thousand people, paying a shilling a time, came to see this unlikely spectacle. Sponsorship deals with leading brands were also vigorously pursued, with Rizla and Philishave supplying prizes for fag-rolling and shaving competitions, respectively.

Arguably the most notorious component of Butlin's camps, the Redcoats, did not feature in Butlin's original plans but arose out of necessity. During the first few days of Skegness it had become patently obvious that the campers were at a loss to know what to do with themselves. And accordingly, left to their own devices, they did little and moped about. Feeling bored and isolated from each other, they also retreated, as English people will, into their own shells. Or clung to their own groups and didn't mingle. Desperate to lift this gloom, Butlin's associate Norman Bradford took a microphone and began joshing with the campers. The patter was greeted so enthusiastically that he made it a regular part of each day's schedule and, at Butlin's suggestion, also adopted a distinctive uniform of a red blazer and white flannels.

Tasked with putting the campers at their ease ('swanning' in Butlin's parlance), performing comic and musical turns, refereeing sporting tournaments, setting up competitions and retaining a cheery disposition even when the little Beaver Club kids were throwing you into the swimming pool, the Redcoats acted as an emollient, oiling the social motor of the camp. Though intended to be friendly enablers, boosting camp spirit by encouraging group participation, their brand of coercion – happy clappy in the manner of stage school kids and religious converts – was deemed sinisterly authoritarian by some. But back in an era when buses had conductors, beaches deckchair attendants and few areas of public space were free from either a guiding human presence or an officious jobsworth, they were generally admired more than reviled. And Redcoats of a certain vintage are prone to swell with pride when recalling the esteem the uniform conferred upon them. Imbuing the blazer with almost magical qualities, they describe it as 'making them somebody else'. Speaking in hushed tones, and with the odd wink and nudge, they mention the admiring glances gained. And then stress they worked from 8 a.m. and 'til eleven or midnight six days a week, weren't allowed to be seen drinking in the bars and always 'played safe' with the campers, because to do otherwise was to run the risk of the sack.

When the boss was around, even campers were not immune from summary dismissal. One morning, catching what he thought was a gardener loafing about on a spade, Butlin issued the man with his marching orders, only to discover that it was a guest offering some friendly advice on bedding plants to an employee. Butlin was a man of exacting standards.

Later tarred with a reputation for dishing up low-brow 'shiniest bald head' contests and 'glamorous granny' competitions, in their infancy and in the immediate post-World War Two years, the camps strove to exude class. That every camp was divided into houses with such regal names as Gloucester and Kent was a deliberate aping of the public school system. And although Butlin reputedly lifted it off the front of a fairground organ, the slogan that adorned every camp clock tower – 'Our One True Intent Is All For Your Delight' – hailed from *A Midsummer Night's Dream*.

When the foundations for Skegness were being laid in 1935, a big-budget Hollywood version of this Shakespearian comedy, starring James Cagney as Bottom and Mickey Rooney as Puck, was doing the rounds. Butlin would similarly experiment with bringing classics to the masses after the war. In tempting the Old Vic Shakespeare Company to Filey and hiring the San Carlo Opera Company from Naples to give touring productions of Puccini's *La Bohème* in 1948, he was tapping into a prevalent feeling that background should no longer be an obstacle to any of the better things of life. In the end, such upper-crust entertainments proved of limited appeal to Butlins regulars. Given the option, they tended to prefer a jolly dance band to the death cries of Desdemona and a funny comic over the emotive warblings in Italian of Left Bank waifs and strays, and forays into high art were all but abandoned by the 1950s.

Having suffered the war and Cripps's austerity measures, the bulk of the nation just wanted a damned good time. No longer willing to be lectured by their supposed betters and with virtually full employment and some 96 per cent of manual labourers in Britain entitled to two weeks' holiday with pay by 1955, the time and the means of doing what pleased you finally became an option for the majority of the population. And reassured by the presence of others, and attuned by the war, national service and unionised workplaces to acting in large-scale groups anyway, campers felt justified in letting themselves go once they'd got through the gates. As contrary as it might seem, in turning themselves over to the confines of the camp, abiding by the early morning 'wakey wakey' calls and joining in with the high jinks on offer, they gained a sense of release. Women, in particular, were spared some of the domestic chores of the rest of the year.

Since birth rates had also soared since the war, the holiday camp, as a package, was almost uniquely suited to meet the needs of the nuclear family in this atomic age. But the maiden flight of the de Havilland Comet from London to Johannesburg in 1952 was an omen of the paradigmatic shift in holiday habits to come. While remaining open only to a privileged minority for years yet, the predilections of the international jet set were soon enough being beamed into living rooms on television shows such as *Whicker's World*. At Butlins the exotic could, nevertheless, be sampled vicariously. Its 'Beachcomber' and 'South Sea' bars putting the ambience of a Rodgers and Hammerstein big-screen outing, if perhaps not Polynesia itself, within easy reach. If contemporary John Hinde postcards are to be believed, sitting on a bamboo chair, you could indulge in some Happy Talking as garlanded and grass-skirted blondes conveyed pints of bitter, in jugs, to your table.

In images like these, luridly coloured and heavily stylised, such incongruities have a special poignancy, signposting the gulf between reality and fantasy. Likewise, in a shot of the French Bar at Filey, it is the beer taps offering Skol lager, Worthington Green Shield and Bass Blue Triangle that nail it to an England where Brigitte Bardot could be a pinup but garlic treated to a wide berth. And it is a cruel irony that camps that were partly created in response to the English weather, and that did so much to foster dreams of internationally-flavoured pleasure, should be abandoned for the hot spots of Benidorm and Marbella.

Where rivals were shifting into self-catering and, in the case of Pontin's, branching out in Europe with Go Pontinental! offshoots on the beaches of Sardinia, Torremolinos and Majorca, Butlin was slower off the mark. Though he'd bag the catering contract for the revolving restaurant at the top of the GPO Tower when Tony 'Wedgie the Whizz' Benn opened it in 1966, he was failing to keep pace with the times. The youngsters that had once been happy enough to watch one of Uncle Boko's magic shows with mother, awed by the fez-wearing prestidigitator's mastery of coins and balls, had grown up and were demanding their own diversions. Only a decade after Cliff Richard's singing had been judged 'too wild' by the bar staff at Clacton, gangs of teenagers were tearing up the camps and holding drunken orgies in the chalets. Their group bookings had to be banned. Extremely reluctantly, Butlin passed the chairmanship of the company to his son, Bobby, on 1 April 1968.

The business was later sold to the Rank Group.

Although Butlins achieved record bookings in 1971 and the number of holidays taken in Britain wouldn't reach their peak until 1974, the historical imperative of the camps was over by the late 1960s. Rising car ownership and an emerging generation who sought to differentiate themselves from both their forebears and their peers through superior consumption, were making them an increasingly anachronistic destination. By then, though, the tide was also turning on the English seaside resort. And while those who were casting their nets elsewhere might not have realised it, Butlin, dubbed 'the Beveridge of Leisure' by Ray Gosling, had probably done more than anyone else to draw attention to its shortcomings.

6
The Good Life

*The Past is a Foreign Country – Westward Ho!
– Du Maurier's Vanishing Cornwall – Cornwall
for the Cornish – Schooled in St Ives*

Nostalgia, as a tired and tiresome joke goes, is not what it used to be. In the good old days there was, for example, a television variety show called *The Good Old Days*. Hosted by Leonard Sachs and featuring such leading lights of contemporary light entertainment as Reg Varney, Eartha Kitt, Morecambe and Wise, Rod Hull, Roy Castle, Frank Carson, Les Dawson and Charlie Williams all dolled-up in Edwardian costumes (as, incidentally, were the audience) and performing music hall turns, it entertained viewers for over thirty years.[22] Finally axed in 1983, its run certainly equalled, if not well exceeded, the period it supposedly harked back to.

Hard as it might be to believe today, it was such a mainstay of the schedule that its absence was once almost unimaginable. Like pound notes, Routemaster buses or Woolworths, it was just *there*. Its very there-ness scarcely needed backing up with any empirical evidence. Much as with *Last of the Summer Wine* at present, it was taken for granted. Even in these days of three television channels and limited repeats, it was bound to be *on* somewhere or soon. And it was almost unfailingly *on* in the homes of elderly relatives visited on days out or over Christmas or on summer holidays.

And then of course, *The Good Old Days* were gone. Ousted by Wogan or Noel Edmond's *Late, Late Breakfast Show* or similar, god knows. But this exercise in nostalgia was itself now capable of being remembered fondly. Which

---

22 This is 'the telly' that the hapless Archie Rice in *The Entertainer* has 'never been on'. In selecting Varney, Dawson et al., over other former household names such as Betty Jumel, Ted Ray or Tessie O'Shea, I am aware I have deliberately chosen performers, though long gone, who continue to have some kind of nostalgic currency today.

was perhaps all it could ever have wished for, actually. Though as it recedes further and further into the past, it becomes harder to believe many people remember it at all. Let alone fondly. I hated it as a child. But it is, of course, part of my childhood memories and isn't easy to forget, however forgetful I increasingly become. With that forget-fulness comes a degree of fondness, regardless of how terri-ble it might actually have been. Certain seaside trips also fall into this category for the same reasons, and, I suspect, must do for almost everyone in this land.

Nevertheless, a world that had space for a prime time TV show given over to the Old Bull and Bush singalongs seems, if anything, far more distant in the twenty-first century than the gap between the Edwardians and then. And today's yesteryear (for which you could insert 1950s and 60s light entertainment stars, beach huts and Audi Quattro sports cars, say) is obviously something quite different again. But both reveal at least as much about the obsessions of their particular presents as the past.

Back in 1930, the Belgian poet but British resident Émile Cammaerts commented that for the English the present was not a hard line of demarcation between two oppo-site worlds but 'a gentle mist through which we wandered leisurely'. Cammaerts also added that he felt the nation travelled through time, as it did through space, dragging behind it 'a quantity of useless luggage'. Which is true enough, though surely true of a great many other nations, too. But it also devalues the special usefulness, not least in matters of leisure, of that baggage to the English – maso-chistically, if nothing else. And masochism, despite its Germanic name, is something the English do rather enjoy.

The past is not, as L.P. Hartley famously put it in *The Go-Between*, a foreign country as such. Though sometimes it can indeed feel more like an entirely lost continent. It is one of the things we regularly deploy, if selectively, to make our own country what it is at any given moment. (Even complete historical amnesia is a willed, or sometimes possibly willful, act of sorts.)[23] One of its greatest assets is its ability to help turn what we actually have into a 'foreign' – and usually far more enchanting, and interesting – country. Or certainly a country where, as when going abroad, there's stuff to discover and the distance from our own common experience is that much more vivid.

Part of the appeal of the seaside for the Romantics was that it remained fairly undeveloped, at least to begin with, and was therefore a much more otherly and historical place. The urge to re-engage with that kind of coastal mystery was to reassert itself again but on a far larger scale in the late 1950s and 60s.

If predominantly (but not exclusively) working-class holidaymakers had been drawn to Butlin's camps and their ilk in the post-war era because they felt they were an improvement on the typical seaside offering, so their middle-class (and upper-working-class) counterparts (of a self-improving bent anyway, and living in a society that thanks to sociologist David Riesman et al.'s popular 1953 bestseller *The Lonely Crowd* was concerned about 'the

---

23 Hartley's first novel, *The Shrimp and Anemone* was, like his best-known later book, an evocation of the loss of childhood innocence one Edwardian summer. Set in Anchorstone, a fictional version of Hunstanton, it was written during the opening years of the Second World War when only a few choppy waves of the North Sea stood between the Norfolk coast and Nazi-occupied Holland.

problem of conformity') also wanted holidays that reflected their increasingly individualistic, and faintly autodidactic, aspirations.

There was nothing especially new about this, but the formation of the Welfare State and the passing of the Butler Education Act, along with increased incomes, an expansion of the range of white-collar jobs and rising levels of homeownership were producing a healthier, better educated, wealthier and more mobile population. One that expected the best for themselves and had less truck with the self-denying pieties of their forebears. They wanted to live enriched and more fulfilling lives and organised their leisure time accordingly. Reductions for most in the hours of a working week meant that these were also boon years for hobbyists – and the English, as Orwell noted in 1941, have always been rather addicted to hobbies. Thousands more now possessed the space, time, money and opportunities to indulge a whim for watercolour painting, gourmet cooking or country dancing, as they saw fit.

As a comic character with short-lived enthusiasms and rather pitiable intellectual and social pretensions, Anthony Aloysius St John Hancock, the thwarted, self-proclaimed genius of 23 Railway Cuttings, East Cheam, who first appeared on radio in 1954, was truly the clown for his time. Tony Hancock, the actor, was himself raised in Bournemouth, starred as a beleaguered beach professor in his film *The Punch and Judy Man* and made one of his last performances on British television compèring a variety show from the ABC Theatre Blackpool in 1966. But the numbers of those now passing up on the full English (pier, prom, sands, winter garden etc.) option was high enough by the early 1960s to be notable. Being unconventional, if only mildly so, was on the road to becoming its own convention.

At this point, the prohibitive cost of flights and restrictions on foreign currency, some elements of which lasted until the early 1970s, put a crimper on overseas travel for the vast majority of British people. But as one of the most geologically rugged and previously more obscure, or certainly less easily accessible, areas of the county, the South West was to see its share of the domestic market rise exponentially. In what the historian Julian Demetriadi refers to as a 'geographical redistribution' of holidaying in the UK, it gained at the expense of more obviously seaside-y spots, particularly in the South East. Between 1951 and 1971, while other coastal areas generally experienced a decline in demand for accommodation, 'an additional 751 hotels' were built in the South West. In 1969, the trade journal *Catering Times* claimed that the region was a 'bigger money-spinning tourist area than Wales, Scotland and Ireland', all places whose visitor numbers had risen as the Brits embraced a greater type and variety of holidays and destinations.

One of the most substantial factors in the advancing popularity of the area to tourists was the opening of the Tamar suspension bridge between Saltash in Cornwall and Plymouth in Devon to traffic in 1961. And that same year, the British Travel Association produced a film entitled *Westward Ho!* to promote tourism in the South West.

Narrated by the fruity-voiced Plymouth-born thesp Paul Rogers and top and tailed with a rousing score by Philip Green, the prolific film composer responsible for lending *Carry On Admiral* and *Sea Fury* suitably nautical, musical ballast (cue hornpipe refrain in any opportune scene), it depicts a Cornwall (and bits of Devon and Dorset) of sandy beaches, craggy coves, mossy cliffs and rocky harbours. A region of endless sunny days, dinky boats, whitewashed cottages, beamed inns, thatched eateries and olde worlde curiosity shoppes. One peopled almost exclusively by jovial, pipe-smoking fishermen in caps, ruddy-faced publicans, respectful guesthouse owners, ever-attentive waitresses, painters in oils-splattered smocks and crinkly eyed rustics who never miss an opportunity to show visitors the correct way to line a rod or bottle a matchstick ship. Or, when a pewter tankard of ale is handy, to regale them with yarns about smugglers and the salting of pilchards in days gone by.

As the script constantly underlines with its references to 'agelessness', 'unchanging villages', 'picture book places' and 'fairy whistle stops', King Arthur at Tintagel, King George's men on the prowl around Burgh Island, Drake and bowls at Plymouth Hoe and Thomas Hardy in Dorchester, what is really being sold here is as much a magical trip back in time as a journey through physical space.

Guiding us on this tour along this *Dr Who*-like continuum are two couples who move silently through each scene with exaggerated gestures, like live-action knitting-pattern models. One pair are youthful, sporty, possibly newlyweds, who drive a swingingly with-it red Mini. And the other are in late middle age, and very probably retired. Their vehicle, consequently, is a tubby chrome-grilled, claret and cream saloon that exudes the safe, comfort-over-style practicality of a knobbly-buttoned cardigan from M&S or a good pair of wellies.

Both voyage on, barely meeting another motorist. Pulling up on empty quaysides with little more than a tug of a handbrake, they saunter off to enjoy a run of maritime idylls and amply lubricated seafood lunches. With both a legal drink-driving limit and Barbara Castle's breathalyser lying, at this stage, some six years off, a spirit of ('Dash it all, we are on holiday, aren't we Marjorie?') one-more-for-the-road prevails. A situation possibly only made worse by a clear division of gender roles that assigns the men, no matter how tight, the wheel and the women the passivity of the passenger seat and, if lucky, an occasional chance to squint at the map. The film often feels like an adult version of those reactionary Ladybird picture books for children. *Janet and John Go West*, say, in which the men handle the driving, order drinks, knowledgeably suggest items off menus, pour wine, take photographs, catch fish, steer tillers and point out sites of interest while their wives, decorative to a fault, look on admiringly.

Now, of course, much of this appears merely comically kitsch. It can be savoured knowingly, like an episode of the having-its-cake-and-eating-it retro-soap *Mad Men*, as proof of how far we've come since then. But if we've become blasé about the sexual politics and boozing habits of nearly half a century ago, other more subtle moments serve to remind us how far we really have travelled since then.

One of the most revealing incidents occurs in a reverie about the perfect holiday in a sequence that is accompanied by images of a painter committing a picturesque bay to canvas. Lingering over every syllable, as only an actor who pronounces the word 'off' to rhyme with 'wharf' can,

Rogers lists a trio of alliterative harbours – 'Mouse Hole, Mullion, Megavissey' – that he declares are 'as pretty as a picture'. Just as we are absorbing this demonstrable truth, since a picture in situ is shown for our approval, he suddenly adds, less wistfully, and almost as if being handed a breaking news bulletin, 'all joined by twenty-minute lengths of motor road, no wonder artists flock to Cornwall.'

Then as now, artists, with their easels, oils and complicated amorous and/or childcare arrangements, were probably just as likely to need cars as, say, butchers or haberdashers. And from the Italian Futurists to Richard Prince, the automobile has itself been as much an object of artistic fascination as the flower or the bowl of fruit. Nevertheless, the combination of the words 'artists', 'Cornwall' and 'motor road', no matter how quaint the latter phrase now sounds, still strikes rather a jarring note. Although it's worth remembering that these same three elements were also what launched John Betjeman's *Shell Guides* back in 1934, despite the fact that the future Poet Laureate omitted St Ives, Cornwall's answer to Montmartre, in his opening volume on the country in the series. But the implication that, in a sense, every budding Frank Bramley is a Mr Toad seems slightly distasteful somehow. Yet this little detail provides the rest of the cheery fantasy with real verisimilitude. Here, in essence, is the mid-twentieth-century dream of the car as the means of discovering the undiscovered for yourself, and the consequence-free liberator of creative potential.

The British B-road, as anaemic a beast in comparison with the highways of America as, say Tommy Steele or Cliff Richard were to Elvis Presley and Jerry Lee Lewis in rock 'n' roll, might not inspire a kinetic rhapsody like *On the Road*. (Races to the coast on this side of the pond were more likely to stir up thoughts of Kenneth More and Larry Adler than Jack Kerouac and Charlie Parker. Though in 1960, councillors in Newquay did attempt to ban a group of 'beatniks' from their town.) But with the wheel of an Austin Countryman, a Morris Traveller or possibly even a more resolutely pioneering Triumph Mayflower in your hands, a full pipe of shag clamped in your teeth, the wife at your side, a hamper full of Spam in the boot and a tartan blanket and a spaniel on the backseat, the motorist of the 1950s could feel at one with the wandering tinkers and painted wagons of an older Romantic tradition. And the Gypsy spirit was alive and well in the English suburbs. Cyril and Doris from Dagenham or Didsbury could play at being Don José and Carmen for a weekend by bolting an Alperson Sprite Caravan – yours for less than £200 in 1959 – to the rear of their car.

By the time of *Westward Ho!*'s release the M1 motorway had been open for two years and the number of licensed cars in Britain was edging up, bumper by bumper, to nine million, an increase of over six million on the previous decade. In London alone the number of private vehicles registered in the 1950s almost doubled from 480,300 to 802,600. Motoring was a mass-market phenomenon. With the transport minister and former road construction company owner, Ernest Marples, covering ever greater swathes of the English countryside in asphalt, the unspoiled lane, the off the beaten track and the out of the way place grew easier to reach and therefore rarer and more desirable. *Westward Ho!*, in many respects, is a rehearsal for much that was to come.

Though it is on a par with the kind of faintly jingoistic off-the-peg Blighty peddled by the Festival of Britain exactly a decade earlier, it sums up, in its own way, a distinct yearning in the period for the accoutrements of yesteryear. A yearning that would only intensify in the face of rapid and often uncertain and unsettling change. On the one hand, this would manifest itself with the formation of historical re-enactment societies like the Sealed Knot and in television programmes such as *Out of Town* and *Going for A Song*, (the precursor to *Antiques Roadshow)* and *The Good Old Days*. And on the other, it can be tracked in the reclamation by the middle classes of Georgian and early-Victorian slum-housing stock set for demolition and handmade-looking farmhouse tables doing a roaring trade in Heal's.

To a nation still struggling to come to terms with its loss of prestige post-Suez, history, or historic myths, would prove an enormous comfort. And, as the American sanctioned Swinging London fandango later exemplified, a heavily stylised version of England that was part David Frost, part Dick Turpin with a dollop of James Bond and Dick van Dyke cockney for good measure, was a highly marketable tourist commodity.

Painted in 1961, Derek Boshier's Pop Art masterpiece 'England's Glory', a witty Americanising of the famous nautical match brand, provides a neat satire of these anxieties. At a push it could almost serve as a commentary on *Westward Ho!* and the emergence of a heritage Britain of England-by-the-pound ploughman's lunches, warm beer and bobbies on bicycles, (two-by-two). That daily life was now heavier on self-service catering, Watney's Red Barrel and *Z cars* only added grist to the mill.

What can really be glimpsed in *Westward Ho!* is tourism inextricably bending virtually everything in the region to its will. Even fishing, along with tin a mainstay of the Cornish economy for centuries, seems to teeter on the brink of becoming a flank of the leisure industry – and long before Thatcherism touted the service economy as an article of ideological faith. 'The fishermen seem unaware that their sleepy village has become a holiday haven', Rogers' voiceover maintains at one point. This is disingenuous in the extreme since these selfsame oblivious-of-visitors sea dogs, are then pictured escorting the younger couple on a mackerel-spinning boat trip from Mevagissey harbour. And just six years later, Daphne Du Maurier would report in *Vanishing Cornwall* that, 'Today the Mevagissey canning factories talk of closing down, not they say, because pilchards are no more but because the fishermen do not care to look for them, declaring that it is not worth their while. They can make more money filling their boats with summer visitors.'

This is, of course, the central bind for tourists seeking the untarnished beach or the eye-pleasing working fishing village the globe over. Their presence inevitably alters the environment. Like a reverse King Midas touch, they often end up killing off what they found most charmingly authentic about a place to begin with. Though given the arduousness of fishing, you can't blame Captain Haddock and his crew for downing their nets when an easier way to make a buck presented itself. And the shoals of pilchards that were once so plentiful that they were salted and exported in their millions by the barrel to Italy and Spain had grown scarcer and scarcer. The last great harvests were recorded in the opening years of the twentieth century; the fish after that and for reasons no one can quite fathom, spawning and feeding further away from the Cornish coast and off into the Atlantic.

But for the likes of Daphne Du Maurier and John Betjeman, such developments were perhaps doubly galling. In hymning its unique character in guidebooks, fiction, verse, prose and on the radio, film and, later, television, they'd probably done as much as anyone else to persuade trippers to visit after the Second War. (And there's nothing like calling a book, *Vanishing X*, or *Lost Y*, to persuade folk to have a poke around the wreckage.)

The hanging pub sign of Jamaica Inn, the former coaching hostelry and temperance house near Launceston immortalised as a smugglers' den by Du Maurier in the eponymous novel (later filmed with a fearsome opening wrecking scene by Alfred Hitchcock), naturally enough, puts in an appearance in *Westward Ho!* Ramping up the mood during this particular sequence, a kind of excise-dodgers montage, Rogers adopts a West Country twang and breaks into a recital of Rudyard Kipling's 'A Smuggler's Song'. The actor, obviously relishing the chance to impart a bit of locally sourced colour, squawks and ooh arrs his way through the poem like a parrot after a night on the slop trays or a Wurzel in desperate need of a key for his brand new combine harvester. That this could well be Rogers' original accent (or one that he imbibed as a child, at least) only makes his delivery more perturbing, since it sounds so ludicrously put on. Though for cinema audiences of the day for whom Robert Newton (cast against type as an undercover excise man in Hitchcock's *Jamaica Inn* but never willingly passing up a chance to roll an 'r' or swivel his eyes as the peg-legged Long John Silver in Disney's full-colour *Treasure Island* of 1950) was the definitive nautical baddy, it may possibly have sounded, if anything, under-done. But then most visitors to the West went, as they had done for a century, expecting to find both character – and characters – and the more primitive-looking the better, no matter how ersatz.

Needless to say, such faux Kernow did not exactly endear itself to Betjeman. As early as 1949, the poet was already complaining about a souvenir shop, previously a jewellers, in his beloved Padstow – a town he revered as 'an ancient, unobvious place' – being kitted out with new 'old' wood beams to enhance its air of antiquity. If unabashedly modern bungalows in Looe with their 'detestable red roofs . . . so ugly in the slate and granite of old Cornwall' were to prove no more acceptable to the poet, then the former was at least in keeping, however dubiously, with the atavistic impulses of a region that to this day holds the not-entirely issue-free Mummers' (or Darkies') Day and the 'Obby 'Oss parade each winter and summer. That each of these 'traditions' in their present form can only be conclusively traced back to the nineteenth century means that they themselves are likely to be Victorian tidy-ups (or embellishments) of less seemly ancient rites, rather like Morris dancing, say.

Which isn't to say that there weren't weird old things to be found in Cornwall in the nineteenth century. There obviously were, it remains an old and an odd place. But what was preserved and subsequently came down to us frequently reflects the predilections of writers, folklor-ists and antiquarians. While evangelical about local ritu-als, myths and superstitions, the knapsack and notebook brigade had their personal quirks. Often amateurs, in the noblest and original, sense of the word, drawn from the ranks of watercolourists, retired schoolmasters and bored churchmen who filled the dark hours scribbling articles for local newspapers and small periodicals, they were prone to be selective, exaggerating here and editing there, as they attempted to document customs that were in many instances on the verge of extinction. The feeling that they alone had the 'in' on something that was very possibly on the way out, probably didn't help. The significance of their own particular discoveries and an amping up of the sheer untouched wildness of what they were describing, being more often than not the result.

In an updated edition of Wilkie Collins's Cornish travelogue *Rambles Beyond Railways*, a book that in 1851 was itself rather guilty of playing up the region's geographic obscurity for Romantic effect (in the view of one later critic, Collins chose to 'shut his eyes to the fact that the railway from Hayle to Redruth had been carrying passengers in quaint little wagons for at least seven years'), the author of *The Moonstone* notes, enthusiastically, that 'two gentlemen' were in the process of restoring the prehistoric stone ruins at St Cleer's wall 'exactly following the original design'. That Collins draws attention to their social rank and stresses their commitment to historical authenticity is as striking as the news of this ancient monument's actual reconstruction in the 1860s.

As Du Maurier was to observe a century later, again in *Vanishing Cornwall*, 'the hard truth' was that 'the preservers' of her own time were 'not always the indigenous but too often sculptors, artists, writers, craftsmen together with the elderly, the retired, the people who came to settle and put down roots; with their opponents more recent newcomers, viewing the coast about them with a speculative eye.'

Today the concept of gentrification is well-worn, the formula of artistic types moving into a neglected area and, in time, encouraging the monied and then the merely curious to follow has such a precedent that it is now pursued as official regional development policy. The sociologist Michael Thompson, who worked as a builder's mate in Islington while completing his PhD, chronicled its emergence in his book *Rubbish Theory*. Based on his firsthand experiences of 'transforming', as he puts it, 'dilapidated early-Victorian artisans' cottages into trendy residencies for *Observer* journalists', Thompson pegs the phenomenon to the early 1960s – only shortly after the malicious destruction of Philip Hardwick's Doric arch at Euston Station highlighted for many the unremitting barbarism of contemporary town planning.

Already mocked by one *Observer* journalist, Michael Frayn, in his Fleet Street novel *Towards the End of Morning* in 1967 and anatomised in savage detail some seven years later by Jonathan Raban in his peerless study of metropolitan life, *Soft City*, gentrification had gone properly coastal by 1975, the year that saw the appearance of Malcolm Bradbury's caustic satire of campus life *The History Man*. Its central characters, Howard Kirk, the libidinous, radical academic, and his free-spirited wife Barbara, take possession of a formerly condemned Georgian property in Watermouth. This seaside town, loosely modelled on Brighton, is home to a progressive university where Howard teaches sociology. Architecturally, and tellingly in contrast to the radical couple's own home, this seat of learning is a shrine to concrete modernism.

But as Du Maurier's comments suggest, these patterns, albeit in a more intensely touristic vein, were equally clearly observable in Cornwall in the 1960s. In 1964, the *Cornish Magazine*, for example, began to produce a regular property supplement, *Homes in Cornwall*, a publication proffering 'homes to suit everyone' from 'the Cornishmen who need new homes for growing families to the welcome immigrant from "up-country" who finds Cornwall an ideal country to live and work or just to retire to.' Curiously, what is missing in this opening editorial, aside from Cornish women, is any specific mention of holiday or second homes per se. But the appearance of phrases like 'ideal summer retreat' in adverts in subsequent editions speak for themselves. By 2005 over six per cent of all homes in Cornwall were estimated to be second homes; on the Isle of Scilly this figure was as high as 25 per cent. While surveys conducted in Manaccan and Portscatho suggested that between 80 and 85 per cent of the properties in these two villages alone were unoccupied for most of the year. In Padstow, dubbed Padstein due to the presence, by 2010, of four Rick Stein fish restaurants, three shops and the Stein cookery school, one in four houses is a second home.

With local wages running at 25 per cent below the national average and house prices commonly the equal of some districts in London, Cornwall has been identified by the homeless charity Shelter as possessing 'the worst affordability gap in the country'. Warnings about Cornwall falling victim to second-home syndrome can be found at least seventy years earlier, however. Sir Arthur Quiller-Couch or

'Q' the Cornish-born editor of the *Oxford Book of English Verse* and the author of a series of historical adventure novels set around Fowey whose titles alone (*Dead Man's Rock*, *The Splendid Spur* and *The Astonishing History of Troy Town* etc.) reek of swashbuckling and mainbrace-splicing derring-do, raised the matter in 1936.

'Worst of all', he wrote, 'is the man who, coming to a beauty-spot with some money in his pocket, tells himself – "what a charming place for a pied-a-terre which I can use in July-August . . ." The process began with his securing a cottage by outbidding a young couple of 'natives' eager to marry and set up house in the one cottage to let within their reach . . .'

The plight of such 'natives' took on an extra dimension in 1951 with the formation of Mebyon Kernow (The Sons of Cornwall), a pressure group and later a political party, dedicated to seeking self-government, promoting the Cornish language and preserving Cornwall's distinct identity and customs. The cry of 'Cornwall for the Cornish' was to supply the prolific writer Denys Val Baker, a long-term resident of Cornwall if not technically a Cornishman himself, with the title of a comic radio play for the BBC in 1964.

Set two years into the future, Val Baker's drama chronicled the failed Cornish War of Independence of 1966. The rebellion in question, it eventually emerges, came unstuck because The League of Landladies, Landlords and Bed & Breakfast Providers entered into a secret pact with the mainland government to allow holidaymakers back into the country. The British forces also cunningly chose to mount their operation to reclaim the nation for

the union on a Thursday afternoon, then half-day closing in Cornwall and when most of the Cornish navy were
off on a smuggling run to the Continent. As a comedy it
has not aged especially. But in gently mocking the isola-
tionist dreams of Cornish nationalists and the rapa-
ciousness of the local hoteliers along with sending up
the sleepiness of life in the country in general, *Cornwall
for the Cornish* conveys a degree of truth and isn't without charm.

Among Val Baker's best-received books, and he
published fourteen novels and twenty-six (largely humor-
ous) autobiographies concerning his family life in
Cornwall alongside hundreds of short stories and radio
plays, was a study of the artistic scene in St Ives, *Britain's
Art Colony By the Sea*. Published in 1959, it appeared
almost exactly thirty years after Ben Nicholson paid
his first visit to St Ives. Painters, like swallows had been
migrating to the small fishing villages of Cornwall for the
summer months ever since the middle years of the nineteenth century. In the 1880s, however, Walter Langley and
Edwin Harris settled in Newlyn, attracted by the harbour,
rough-walled cottages and the profusion of horny-
handed seafaring types, toothless crones and cherub-
faced urchins that they wasted no time in committing to
canvases that were admired for their expressive realism in
their day. Much as Paul Gauguin and Émile Bernard had
lured other painters to Pont-Aven in Brittany, Newlyn
soon became home to a more permanent community of
like-minded artists whose house style was disseminated
by Elizabeth and Stanhope Forbes who set up a painting school in the town. Up to the First World War, when

its critical influence waned sharply, Newlyn remained the epicentre of artistic life in Cornwall.

Nevertheless, Polperro, Mousehole, Newquay, Falmouth and St Ives all had their fair share of artists in residence too. Though most were knocking out politely Romantic marine scenes for retired naval officers to hang in their parlours until Cedric Morris and then Kit Wood and Ben and Winifred Nicholson adopted St Ives in the late 1920s. Their patronage was to make its name virtually synonymous with modernist art, in the process turning it into a destination for other Bohemian urbanites burnt out on the city as a creative stimulus.

At the point when Ben Nicholson 'discovered' St Ives, the artist, heavily influenced by Picasso and Braque, was starting to paint figurative and abstract works that sought to recapture the freshness of primitive art. Alienated by the consequences of what many saw as unfettered technological progress, the primitive was now widely identified with the spiritual by modernists who were also seeking to cast off the dead hand of classicism. In Cornwall, Nicholson not only met a landscape that was more primal but in the local artist Alfred Wallis, he effectively found his noble savage.

Possibly the world's best worst painter, Alfred Wallis could almost be a figure from the pages of *Treasure Island*. Signing on as a cabin boy aged nine, Wallis had spent nearly thirty years at sea before washing up in St Ives in 1890, where he went on to earn a crust, variously, as a rag-and-bone merchant, odd-job man and ice cream vendor. He only took up painting in 1925 at seventy and 'for the company' after his wife's death. It was by pure chance that some three years later, Ben Nicholson and Christopher 'Kit' Wood happened to be strolling along Black Road West on their way back from Porthmeor Beach when they passed a cottage with an open door. Unavoidably glancing in, they spied an array of peculiar paintings executed on scraps of cardboard that were pinned to the interior walls with oversized nails. Nicholson later recalled that these were deployed in inverse proportion to the size of the pictures, with the smallest paintings seeming to be fixed up with the biggest nails and vice versa. Intrigued beyond belief by this unorthodox tableau, the pair knocked on the door.

The Wallis who ushered them in that afternoon was by now living, according to his biographer Sven Berlin, in 'a condition of poverty and filth that was a disgrace to human life.' He was also suffering from what today would probably be diagnosed as the early stages of senile dementia but then was called, simply, madness. Plagued by voices and frequently given to breaking off in mid-sentence to insist that his dead wife pipe down, Wallis was convinced that the Devil had the run of an upstairs room and was plotting to secure his eternal damnation.

His paintings, similarly, represent a reality where the usual borders between the living and the dead, the concrete and the imagined and even the picture and the frame have gone slightly soggy. When discussing his art it is impossible not to talk about its 'naivety' or its 'childlikeness'. And his lighthouses, wobbly penile lollies jutting out of scribbly grey seas at unlikely angles, and twin-masted clippers, little more than kites fixed to muddy blue and black lines, and cottages, rows of lilting boxes laid virtually on top of one another or slithering up hills, are rendered with a sort of artlessness that is breathtakingly childish. Wallis's use of perspective and his idea of composition veer from primitive cave painting to positively medieval. Ships and houses appear as comets in seas that could be skies or scuttle along bottom corners or on side edges like animals in tapestries. Yet cumulatively these 'flaws', for want of a better word, seem so systematic that they become strengths. Time and again, two and sometimes three 'wrongs', somehow combine to form a more than all right picture. Or certainly one that has such an aesthetically appealing coherence of form that it can't easily be dismissed as the work of a child or an inept amateur. Even if the latter might be pretty near the mark.

Wallis employed common house and boat paint for his pictures, resulting in some inventive colour schemes, and painted on whatever was to hand. The back of a GWR Railway timetable. A piece of driftwood. It didn't really matter. But cardboard boxes that he snipped into irregular shapes served as his canvases for the most part.

The shape and texture of what he ended up with also helped to dictate what he painted. A seascape, for instance, might take its line from a skinny strip of card or a schooner could arise on a squat square board. And more often than not a section of the board itself was left untouched and incorporated into the finished pictures. A patch of its original brown, grey, white or green cropping up somewhere in the sky, or in a field or in the ocean.

The subjects of his pictures were, as he put it, 'What used to Bee out of my memory, what we may never see again.' We could perhaps quibble over whether anyone other than Wallis himself ever saw, or even dimly remembered seeing, ships or Cornish fishing ports that looked quite like the ones he painted. But the decision to fill his boards with by now vanished clippers and sailing brigs makes them seem all the more archetypically maritime, while also imbuing them with an oddly ghostly air.

In photographs, Wallis, usually clad in an oversized floppy cap, baggy Guernsey and wide trousers and his long thin nose underscored by a resplendently droopy Zapata moustache, looks more like an Italian partisan than a Cornish hermit as such. Although often a brusque judge of his young admirers' art, (once shown some reproductions of Nicholson's paintings in a copy of *Cahier's d'Art*, he remarked, 'I don't think much o' they') this idiot savant profoundly effected the direction of their subsequent works. It was because of Wallis that the Nicholsons and Wood, accompanied by his mistress Frosca Munster, moved to St Ives. Wood visited Wallis almost daily, spending hours studying his technique and putting a little of the insane old man's methods to work in his own paintings. Nicholson too, now began to deploy what he later called, a 'cultivated artlessness' that ultimately lead him to full-blown abstraction.

Wood was to die at 29 in 1930. Possibly suffering from withdrawal symptoms to an addiction to opium, he threw himself under a train at Salisbury station. While Wallis, eventually so unable to cope with the strain of daily living that his cottage became overrun with vermin, was interned in an institution at Madron a decade later and died of 'senile decay' in 1942. Leaving Nicholson and his second wife, Barbara Hepworth, and their acolytes to carry the torch for St Ives after the Second War.

Nicholson would abandon St Ives for Switzerland in 1958 – just before Val Denys's book was published. And by the early 1960s the St Ives school itself was on the wane, its circle squared by the throngs of budding painters in the vein of the weekenders from *Westward Ho!* (or Tony Hancock in *The Rebel*) beating a path there and for whom Wallis, arguably, rather than Wood or Nicholson, was in a sense their guiding light and patron saint.

7
Fighting on the Beaches

*Margate Meltdown – Graham Greene and
Pinkie Brown – Damn You Weymouth – Rods
and Mockers – Too Cool in Clacton*

As fabrics go, black leather never looks especially comfortable on a hot day by the sea. What could be cosy enough in winter, in the rain, or, one imagines, when worn roaring along on a motorbike, exposed to all the elements on offer and at high speed, screams 'clammy' when at rest and smouldering, perhaps just a touch, under a harsh midday sun.

Its sartorial unsuitability as jobbing beachwear, it seems to me, is also only underlined by the omnipresence of ice cream. Whatever the hard science, and I am willing to accept that wearing leather on a hot day, counterintuitively, might actually lower the body temperature, much as drinking a mug of steaming tea is supposed to, and that eating ice cream could have the opposite effect, but . . . but . . . the snowy peak of a Mr Whippy, say, never strikes one as more cooling than when set beside the boiling-tar blackness of most biker clobber. And on an almost unfeasibly warm Bank Holiday Monday in May 2009, a large crowd of bikers was to be spied on Margate's harbourside all dressed in leather, and a good percentage lapping away at ice creams as if their internal thermostats had gone haywire. With the ocean so near to hand and carrying crash helmets under their arms, they looked like deep sea divers from earlier times. Clomping about in bulky boots and weaving slightly unsteadily along the crowded narrow causeway, you could believe they'd just been winched out of the water en masse and were still getting reacquainted with dry land. This, however, was Margate Meltdown, a rally for motorcycling enthusiasts organised by the Ace Cafe. Once the favourite haunt of the Ton Up kids in the 50s and 60s, this formerly defunct greasy spoon at Stonebridge on the North Circular was revived in typically late 1990s style, as a retro rocker cafe-bar, club and outside events promoter with a covetable and no doubt profitable line in Ace logo branded t-shirts, sweat-tops, badges, mugs, stickers, pencils what-have-you. (Its website homepage springs into life with the slogan, 'Welcome to the Legend' before extorting browsers to 'Fire it Up!')

Margate is a resort that has suffered more than most since cheap Continental package deals, with their promise of sun, sea and sangria or at the very least sunburn, lager and chips, began spiriting indigenous holiday crowds away. The boarded up shops. The giant seafront water slide so decayed that it resembles a vast Bacon Frazzle crisp. The paint on the railings blistered and peeling like a snake shedding its skin, and dotted with liver spots of rust. The Lido reduced to a tatty concrete meniscus, covered in sand and weeds. The missing letter 'y' on the Margate Yacht Club sign. Like the names appliquéd on local girl Tracey Emin's tent, all of these little details, and many more, tell you how fucked the place has been since the 1970s. And just now it was suffering the added indignity of having some of Alan Sugar's paperclip minders try their hands at rebranding it in weekly instalments. And on national TV.

Today, though, Margate had run up the flags and dug out the bunting for the Ace gang and was reaping the rewards: the sun was out and people were in. Local councillors and civic dignitaries in smart dress were to be seen pacing about the throng. Beaming at small children with balloons and fat hairy greasers in oily denim and leather cowboy hats alike, they inspected the bikes parked on the prom, taking pains to stop here and there and gesture admiringly at a particularly long and shiny pair of front wheel forks or an especially fascinating gas tank custom paint job depicting a flame-haired Jezebel in a state of semi-undress. One or two clearly still yearned for the days when they could have pinned a rosette on something or raffled some jam.

On a stage in the main harbour square a trio of musicians (two resplendently be-quiffed, one with the pate – and build – of Uncle Fester), were belting out old rockabilly numbers. The antiquated sounds of their double bass, drums and tinny electric guitar floated down to the foreshore, mingling with a sine wave of gunned motorbike engines to create an eerie approximation of a 1950s novelty hit about teenage road deaths. This cacophony was to serenade the arrival of a small crocodile of Mods on mirror-bedecked scooters. Desert boot and green army parka clad emissaries from the Deal scooter club, 'the real Deal' as Pete, one of its chief commissars quipped, they came in peace. 'Anyone on two wheels at the weekend' Pete stated, 'is good to us.' And stowing their Vespas in between a Triumph Bonneville with a petrol tank as engorged as a python ingesting a mongoose, and an Enfield ('sadly a modern Indian knock off' as someone rather disappointedly noted), any stylistic differences quickly slipped away, and a hearty bonhomie akin to that found at Remembrance Day parades among ex-servicemen once on opposing sides was palpable.

Though perhaps a closer analogy is really that of battle re-enactments. A touch of The Sealed Knot meets

Quadrophenia, with each group on this day donning historical costumes but eschewing the striding around the muddy fields play-fighting with pikestaffs nonsense in favour of swapping anecdotes about the best chrome polishes, maximum torques and valves per cylinder layouts.

Many of those here, in any case, were far too young to have been around when *Quadrophenia* was released let alone taken part in the Mods vs Rockers rucks of forty-five years ago. That such a concord should exist between these now-aged youth cults and the good burghers of Margate would have been almost unimaginable then. Back in the 1960s, a group of some sixty local traders led an ultimately unsuccessful but highly orchestrated campaign to enact legislation to prevent Mods and Rockers from entering seaside resorts. And following scrums over the Whitsun Bank Holiday in 1964, it was the Margate magistrate Dr George Simpson, breezily dishing out hefty fifty-quid fines to practically anyone bundled into the back of a Black Maria that weekend, who delivered one of the most incendiary speeches of the period. A speech that was seized upon like manna from heaven by the press. The boys in Fleet Street proving then as now, ever eager to stoke the nation's hangers-and-floggers into a frenzy of mass indignation during the slow news days of a Bank Holiday period. We can surely picture the scene at a million breakfast tables up and down the land: after Lady Chatterley, Profumo, The Beatles et al., already-disgusted of Acacia Avenue, sits in shirtsleeves, braces, a Rotary Club tie in a Windsor knot, his moral outrage growing with every line read and each subsequent sip of tea or mouthful of bacon catching in their throat as the bile rises up from their stomach and sentences about dogs having the run of the country and emigrating to Australia are finally spluttered out with deeper conviction than normal.

Described in the *Daily Express* as 'The Quiet Man Who Rocks The Thugs' and 'a beloved local family doctor for 25 years', Simpson performed to perfection the role of white knight in a light grey suit in this barbarians-at-the-gate Fleet Street melodrama. 'It is unlikely that the air of this town has ever been polluted as it has by the hoards of hooligans we have seen here this weekend', he maintained, choosing to gloss over any recurring problems with sewage on the beaches in the area. 'These long-haired unkempt, mentally unstable, petty little saw-dust Caesars', he offered in a concluding rhetorical flourish, 'could only find courage by hunting like rats in packs.'

The problem of rival tribes of youths dukeing it out on the beaches did not begin in Margate, however, nor Brighton nor Hastings, but in Clacton. And, as with so much else in the story of the English seaside, the weather was by far and away the most significant factor in a phenomenon that initially owed more to the feverish imagination of headline writers than reality as such, anyway.

Rowdy teenagers had, in a sense, been menacing Bank Holiday festivities since their inception in the 1870s. And the capacity for newspapers in England to become indignant about the sight of young people letting off steam at the seaside knew few bounds well before the arrival of Vespas and BSAs on Marine Drive. In a piece headed 'Bournemouth's August Bank Holiday Scandal' from 1938, the *Bournemouth Times* was frothing at the mouth at the mere arrival of 'groups of youths, some wearing gaudy paper hats with inscriptions such as 'Come Up and See Me Sometime', parading along the Drive singing the latest dance hits'.

That same year saw the publication of Graham Greene's *Brighton Rock*, a novel that acknowledged the darker undercurrents of adolescent culture sloshing around the South Coast. Though in the interests of fiction it perhaps whisked the Hoxton Mob, a London razor gang run to ground at the Lewes races in 1936, a little closer to the shoreline than they might have liked. Just as a feller 'from the Wandsworth dog tracks whose face had been carved because he was suspected of grassing to the bogies after a killing at the stadium' was more of an inspiration to Greene than anything he'd witnessed in Brighton.

Its setting was, nonetheless, far from arbitrary. Since Regency times, when prostitutes and pickpockets worked the promenades and smugglers the coves and bays' the seaside has always had its seedier underbelly. Violence also tends to flourish in places where large, anonymous crowds gather on hot (and, indeed, miserably cold) days. A queue for the Ghost Train jumped. A jostled elbow at a seafront bar. An ill-timed suggestion of a nightcap in a nearby hotel to somebody else's wife. The wrong colour shirt. It doesn't take much to flip the English from restrained to needing to be restrained by several officers of the law.

And then, of course, there are the perennial tensions over territory between visitors and residents. The latter often relying upon the former for their livelihood but resenting the servitude of it all the same. Local racketeers, meanwhile, in reserving the right to fleece the innocent and the not so innocent abroad have always taken a rather dim view of outsiders attempting to muscle in on their turf.

Pinkie, though, as Greene's teenage godfather on sea, (especially after he was fixed on celluloid with Richard Attenborough putting in the performance of a career as the sociopathic Catholic gang leader in the Boulting brothers film of 1947) proved an acutely prophetic creation. Part role model for a generation for whom absent fathers and bombed out streets had defined their earliest years, and part archetypical folk devil, Pinkie would come into his own in the 1950s and 1960s. Reborn (or remade) as the unruly juvenile delinquent, in an era of Angry Young Men, Outsiders called Colin and Rebels without Causes, a little of Pinkie was to be spied in the teenage wrong-uns pictured gunning down coppers in *The Blue Lamp* (1950) or impregnating Joan Collins in *Cosh Boy* (1953).

But it is not really until Joseph Losey's 1963 picture *The Damned,* a loose adapted of H.L. Lawrence's science fiction novel *Children of the Light*, that Pinkie's big-screen heirs return to a British beach. Shot in 1961 and around Weymouth, *The Damned* is a genuine oddity. A nuclear-age-anxiety Hammer horror flick, it features a eugenic scientist, a dubious government cum military agency, an avant-garde sculptress, an American tourist, a comely maiden, a tribe of irradiated children and a motorcycle gang. The end of civilization, incest and violence are its themes, and the result is a heady brew of spine-chilling action, armchair-philosophising, portentous futuristic codswallop and attractive coastal cinematography that is as hauntingly magnificent as it is infuriatingly all over the shop. For our purposes, though, it is the timely depiction of Ton Up kids as the social pariahs of a seaside town that is chiefly of interest. The lyrics to the film's theme song, a rather show tune-y imitation of a Bill Haley number supplied by in-house Hammer composer James Bernard and entitled 'Black Leather Rock', fixed the connection between Dorset bikers and untrammelled evil for the viewer with brisk simplicity. Its opening lines run:

> 'Black Leather, Black Leather,
> Smash, Smash, Smash,
> Black Leather, Black Leather,
> Crash, Crash, Crash,
> Black Leather, Black Leather,
> Kill, Kill, Kill . . .'

And the tune, neatly woven into the opening scene of the movie, serves as an immediate overture to violence: kohl-eyed temptress Joan, played with impish guile by Shirley Anne Field, whistles and sings snatches from the chorus as she lures a middle-aged American visitor into a beating by the biker gang. The leader of this pack is her brother, King. A debonair, incestuously inclined but rather asexual psychopath, all too convincingly unhinged in Oliver Reed's glassy-eyed characterisation, King carries an umbrella and sports a tweed jacket and tie. In contrast to the leathers and fairground-prize cowboy hats worn by his troops, sartorially, he appears much more like a Mod than a greaser. But, as we shall see, in the earliest seaside dust ups the battle lines between these two factions were actually far less clear cut than is sometimes supposed.

Here, though both King and his crew are all disparaged as 'Teddy Boys'. And while the vagaries of pop fashion, possibly, took a little longer to reach Weymouth in those days, and the Teds, anachronistic by 1961, were downright embarrassing by the time of the picture's eventual release two years later, their mantle in almost every respect had indeed been passed onto the Rockers. And especially in the general disapprobation heaped upon their heads by the great and the good.

With their endearing faith in a primitive, adolescent musical form that was already far from youthful by the early 1960s, and a style of dress that Marlon Brando had first test driven in *The Wild One* back in 1953 (although stills alone had to suffice in Britain, as the film itself was banned until 1967 on this side of the pond), the Rockers swam quite belligerently against the tide of mainstream culture.

If the Teds had largely exchanged flick-knives for Ford Consuls and relegated their drape coats to the back of the wardrobe by now, then in speeding along on their bikes and holing up with like-minded souls in steamy transport caffs, the jukebox spinning old RCA 45s, the Rockers tapped a gateway to a prelapsarian realm. A realm where Elvis was still King, rather than a sideburn shorn Samson blindly ambling through one bad movie after another, and Gene Vincent was sweetness itself and packing out the Brighton Essoldo each and every night. Motion, far from inducing sickness, was the cure to ills of a humdrum reality. Speed helped to transport them to a higher plane. The roar of a well-tuned engine drowned out the entreaties of parents, teachers, vicars and foremen to make something better of your life, look lively, smarten up, get a haircut, get married, get a house, get rid of that soddin' bike. While smug family after smug family sat, red faced and squirming on the leather upholstery of their Wolseley 6/90s or Austin Westminsters in a Bank Holiday traffic jam, the Rocker roared by on the inside lane. Insouciantly ignoring all but the road ahead as he passed (and in 1964, it was largely he), the Ton Up kid knew that each and every one of those car drivers was cursing him, willing an inopportunely opened van door, a low-lying telegraph cable, a brick wall, anything that could halt and ideally hospitalise, to suddenly appear from nowhere and curtail his ride. And in that millisecond he'd won. The Ton Up could look down on all the people who always looked down on him, and feel bloody good as he thundered around the ring roads. Or for a proper burn up, hared down to the coast.

And in the opinion of the novelist and 1960s Mod, Howard Baker, 'seaside towns were the domain of the rocker, their patch.' Every Rocker, Baker imagined at that time, 'dreamt of working on the dodgems, with the sound of Del Shannon echoing past the helter-skelter.' It was this dream that was memorialised in the nostalgic 1973 rock 'n' roll flick *That'll Be the Day*, where Ringo Starr and David Essex are to be found manning the dodgems on an Isle of Wight funfair to the strains of 'Hats off to Larry' and similar. From the period itself, the score to *A Taste of Honey*, filmed by Tony Richardson in 1961, noticeably slips into ersatz rock when the drama switches, if briefly, from Manchester to Blackpool. Strikingly, this music largely accompanies footage of Helen, a now aging good-time girl with a sulky teenage daughter, and her current swain,

Peter, a dipsomaniac second-hand car dealer a few years her junior, enjoying themselves on the pier amusements and dancing in the ballroom. In linking this type of music to the grown-ups who are incapable of growing up rather than the actual adolescent, it seems to flag up both its age and its immaturity.[24]

The name 'Rocker' too, while tipping its hat to Haley et al., is obviously also a type of chair. One that tobacco-chewing old-timers on porches in cowboy pictures, in particular, are always inordinately attached to. And accordingly, it is quite widely argued, the moniker originally arose as a pejorative thrown at them by Mods. Anyone, in their eyes, who rode a motorbike was either mad (i.e. off their rocker) and/ or seriously out of date. The latter the cardinal sin in a movement committed to being constantly of the moment, the very instant, preferably.

The Mod was a more studiously metropolitan creature. Though often from the same working-class backgrounds and hailing from the same urban or far-flung suburban and even coastal districts as the Rocker, the Mod universe, despite numerous geographical overlaps and an affection for two-wheeled motorised vehicles, revolved around nightclubs and boutiques in Soho and central London. Fleeting stop-offs at the tea stall on Chelsea Bridge and high-speed excursions to the wilds of Box Hill, Hanger Lane and beyond were never going to satisfy any movement with

24 Though as the sequence is a homage of sorts to *O Dreamland*, a documentary portrait of Margate's funfair rather lacking in empathy, directed in 1953 by Richardson's Free Cinema movement colleague Lindsay Anderson, the music could easily be there to underline the tawdriness of the place and Peter and Helen's antics.

Brummel-like displays of narcissism built into its DNA. Where Rockers, although not exclusively, tended to be drawn from the blue-collar world of labourers, mechanics and lathe operators, their look suiting, perfectly, days spent outdoors or with oily rags, the Mods, for the large part, were taken from the class of office boys, shop assistants and bell hops, who had to be smart for work, and prided themselves on being smarter still when out of it.

A fairly early and enthusiastic description of what was called 'the modernist' style appears in *Absolute Beginners*, Colin MacInnes's 1959 novel about coffee bar-haunting London teens in the months leading up to the Notting Hill race riots. MacInnes binds the fashion to his character Dean's love of modern jazz. And in the book, the Modernist's opposite number is not a Rocker but 'a skiffle survival with horrible leanings to trad' jazz called the Misery Kid. From his get-up he sounds like a Ban the Bomb Beat in need of a march, an acoustic guitar and a CND badge to complete the package. Pilloried as a scruffy Herbert, his 'long-brush-less hair', tweed riding jacket, tight striped trousers, grubby collared shirt, 'boots' and 'sausage-rolled umbrella' are laid down in distinctly withering terms.[25] Dean's finicky outfit, on the other hand, is itemised in rather loving detail, and

25 In his memoir about the birth of the counter-culture, *Give the Anarchist a Cigarette*, Mick Farren recalls visiting two friends in Brighton over one of the Bank Holiday weekends in 1964, when the Mods and Rockers were bashing the hell out of each other. He writes, 'As three scruffy non-participants in boots, old army shirts, tight dirty jeans and long unkempt hair, we defied categorisation, but were asked to define ourselves a hell of a lot that day.' He goes on to relate how they narrowly avoided being beaten by both sides by explaining that they were 'Beatniks', to which both Mods and Rockers alike, responded, 'You mean like Bob Die-lan', before leaving them alone.

the love of detail here, as it would be for Mod proper, is very much the point. 'College-boy smooth crop hair with burned-in parting, neat white Italian rounded-collared shirt, short Roman jacket very tailored (two little vents, three buttons), no turn-up narrow trousers with 17 inch bottoms absolute maximum, pointed-toe shoes and white mac.'

MacInnes also describes what their female counterparts would be likely to be wearing, trad' girl going for 'long hair, untidy with long fringes, maybe jeans and a big sloppy sweater' with 'smudged-looking the objective', and Mod girl apparently opting for 'seamless stockings', 'short hemlines', 'short blazer jacket, hair done up into the elfin style' and face pale 'corpse colour with a dash of mauve, plenty of mascara.' Although finessed much further in the next five years with such additions as two-tone or tonic suits, pork pie hats, cycling tops, target t-shirts, desert boots and so on and tights and Quant 'mini' skirts for women, the bones of the Mod look for both sexes are immediately recognisable here.

Continental and, particularly, Italian, tailoring and design were a major component of the look. In television news footage shot at Margate in 1964, a couple of Mods on scooters even appear dressed in stripy Breton-style tops and berets and lack only the string of onions to complete the English stereotype of Gallic national dress. And when not bopping the night away to R&B with the aid of French Blues (drinamyl), the chunter and hiss of the Gaggia machine and endless cups of espresso coffee were staple Mod soundtracks and stimulants.

For all that, though, America had a far greater influence

on Mod fashion than is often acknowledged. The college-cut hairstyle (known in some quarters as 'the Perry Como'), the sporty jumpers, fitted slacks, Hush Puppies suede shoes and striped scarves that many wore, were an Anglicised twist on too-cool-for-school Ivy League preppy gear. (Itself an American take on the tweedy Oxbridge-look.) The preferred fishtail parka was a US Army surplus item that had been designed in 1951 for soldiers serving in Korea. And even that most quintessentially European means of transport, the Vespa, was itself based on American army scooters that Allied troops had driven in Italy at the end of the war. And the Vespa scooter also only really became chic and an emblem of liberated, Continental modernity after Audrey Hepburn and Gregory Peck put one through its paces in the Hollywood movie *Roman Holiday* in 1953.

Like the vintage rock 'n' roll fetishised by the Rockers, Mod music too, was sourced almost exclusively from the States. Ace Faces, or so purists nowadays maintain, were never taken in by local Johnny-come-lately tickets like The Who. The Mod elite listened, or more accurately, danced to black American rhythm and blues, soul and, later, Jamaican blue beat, if they could. Though given the prevalence of fifteen-year-old Modettes clutching Japanese trannies tuned to Radio Caroline – the pirate pop station started broadcasting on the Easter weekend of 1964 – at these coastal gatherings, musical policy was probably, and unavoidably, much less doctrinaire than the earnest keepers of the flame and revivalists like to claim. Youth culture as a living breathing entity, feeling its way, snacking on a variety of external sources and fending off others, is never quite as neat as it latterly appears.

Which, finally, dear reader, brings us back to the little matter of the seaside . . . though we need to look over the Atlantic for a moment. For one of the major changes in the late 1950s and early 60s was a significant shift in teenage fashions and fancies from the East to the West Coast of America. Precipitated by a thriving local economy, fuelled by the defence industry, California became the Golden State. And its sandy beaches and expansive highways, packed with affluent baby-booming teens, birthed a plethora of marine, musical and automotive subcultures that were soon the envy of the world. The lightweight beach flick *Gidget* in 1959 ignited global interest in the relatively obscure Californian sport of surfing. Selling an idyllic vision of endless summer days where 'stacked' bikini-clad honeys and buff, tanned clean-cut dudes frolicked in the warm, crystalline waters of the Pacific Ocean, its formula was mined to death over the next six years or so in such subsequent films as *Beach Party*, *Muscle Beach Party*, *Beach Blanket Bingo*, *How to Stuff A Wild Bikini*, *Beach Ball*, *A Swingin' Summer*, *The Girls on the Beach*, *Wild on the Beach* . . . and I could go on.

The surf fad was to spawn its own brand of instrumental music, characterised by gluggily aquatic-sounding guitars and pioneered by Dick Dale and the Del-Tones. (Dale and co were the house band of the Rendezvous Ballroom in Balboa, a sundown Mecca for Orange County board fiends.) Its esoteric argot, conventions, vehicles and dress codes were further promoted in song by the Beach Boys. Astute surfing carpetbaggers who rode the wave with a brilliantly contrived repertoire of songs championing the sunkissed pleasures of beaches, hot rod cars and girls, the group enjoyed a top twenty hit with 'Surfin' USA' in the UK in 1963 – proving, if nothing, else, how well the form travelled.

And this is the point: while neither UK Mods nor Rockers were devotees of Californian beach culture per se, both groups were well versed in its iconography. Consciously or not, they had internalised notions of youth culture that hailed from the States. Though this was more straightforwardly the case with the Rockers, who directly aped the Hell's Angel motorcycle gangs that had first emerged in California in the late 1940s. (As Hunter S. Thompson noted in his book, *Hell's Angels*, 'the California climate is perfect for motorcycles, as well as surfboards, swimming pools and convertibles.')[26] The Mods were no less susceptible to an idea of beach-based pleasure that, while possibly one third St Tropez, owed more to the parent-free Fun, Fun, Fun of Southern California than the tatty realities of a traditional family resort like Clacton. And poor old Clacton was really to pay simply for disabusing all concerned of that idea.

For reasons that remain fairly obscure, a contingent of about 1,000 Mods from London and the surrounding suburbs opted to hot foot it down to Clacton for the Easter weekend of 1964. That Butlins had a camp just outside the town and that it was a popular destination for cockney

---

26 And incidentally, one of the incidents that made the Hell's Angels so notorious was an alleged gang rape at a beach town called Seaside in California.

day- trippers, may have meant that it induced warm memories of childhood for some teenage Mods.

And while what The Who later termed 'My Generation' were somewhat over-inclined to believe that everything they did represented a seismic break with tradition, the rituals of hitting the seaside of a Bank Holiday were deeply ingrained. (Frankly, where else was there to go?)

In any event, 'the word', or so anyone can seemingly remember, and memories are not strong on this point, had, apparently, gone round the Mod clubs. ('Clacton', wink, wink, a finger conspiratorially tapped on the side of nose, 'you coming?', whatever.) Everyone who was anyone, or anyone who aspired to be anyone, was going. And learning this fact in the small hours and probably pilled up to the eyeballs, the prospect must have seemed mighty appealing. There you were beside the dance floor, the air full of smoke and sweat, a slightly metallic tang lingering in the mouth and the impulse to be impulsive heightened by amphetamines, and bam, someone suggested Clacton. The cogs turned. Fresh Air. Cool water. Hot sun. The beach for a bed. A bag of chips. A likely chance of crumpet. Pinball. More pills. An opportunity to parade some city flash in the provinces. Irresistible. And so off you went. Pills aside, possibly, these thoughts, or ones very much like them, have surely been at the back of almost every seaside day trip taken by the nation's youngsters since Victorian times.

What awaited these particular kids however was a tad disappointing, to put it mildly. Not only was it bloody freezing – and the Easter Sunday that March was to be the coldest on record for eighty years – hardly anything was open yet. And what was open was not especially pleased to see you. Nor your forty mates, all of you with demands for 'eggs, beans, chips, tea, twice, chief' and clammy fists despoiling their immaculately polished countertops. Left with little to do except traipse along the front, the sickly sweet smell of fried onions and candyfloss omnipresent, a certain desperation began to take hold. Scuffles broke out. Punches were thrown – mostly, from what can be gathered, between locals and those down from London. An old lady on the seafront was jostled. The odd beach pebble was thrown through the window of an unobliging cafe or pub. A deckchair or ten were overturned. Those on scooters (most had in fact come down on the coach or by the train) revved their engines and mounted promenade pavements. Flying about like wasps in need of a good swat they attracted the attention of the few Ton Up boys knocking around, who merely to have something to do themselves, duly, if half-heartedly gave chase. Someone fired a starting pistol. And so it went on, until a deployment of stiff-backed coppers with neatly trimmed moustaches and fang-toothed Alsatian dogs arrived to arrest the 'troublemakers' and the whole sorry show was brought to a rather bathetic end.

As the home secretary, Mr Henry Brooke, subsequently called upon to explain the incident to Parliament, put it, 'tempers flared and a certain amount of fighting broke out'. But there was 'nothing like a riot or gang warfare'. And 'Clacton', he stated, quite emphatically, 'was not sacked.' This was not, however, the verdict you would draw from picking up almost any newspaper in the immediate aftermath of the event. 'Day of Terror by Scooter Groups', thundered the *Daily Telegraph* on the Easter Monday.

'Youngsters Beat Up Town – 97 Leather Jacket Arrests' reported a front-page headline in the *Daily Express* on the same date. 'Jail these Wild Ones', demanded the *Daily Mirror*, a day later. And with the *Daily Mail* publishing a handy 'Are You a Mod or A Rocker?' quiz and every Fleet Street hack worth his notebook, trilby and grubby mac digging up quotes about score-settling rematches at Margate and Brighton and remarks about Mods wearing lipstick and smelling the grease on Rockers in the weeks before Whitsun, the following Bank Holiday could hardly fail to kick off. The kids, haplessly, were much like bulls in a ring who are goaded into charging purely to be put to the sword by a brave matador. Such spectacles have the effect of reaffirming who wields the most power, after all.[27]

From a press point of view, Whitsun went like clockwork. In Brighton, packs of Mods and Rockers hared around after one another. Bottles and stones were thrown. Deckchairs were broken up and burned. And a sit-down protest was staged by the Palace Pier when the police attempted to disperse the crowds. In Margate, windows of a hardware shop, a pub and cafe were smashed and later, some thirty youths in leather jackets chanting 'Up the Rockers' were prevented from marching along the prom. 'There was Dad asleep in a deckchair and Mum making sandcastles with the children, when the boys took over the beaches at Margate and Brighton yesterday and smeared the traditional postcard scene with blood and

---

27 Though intriguingly, one pair of Mod girls, interviewed on Carnaby Street for ITN news, were not convinced there'd be trouble a second time round, arguing that the lack of sun at Clacton was the problem and, reasoning, that because Brighton, to their minds, was much sunnier, no one would bother.

violence', was how the *Daily Express* chose to chronicle events on 19 May 1964.

But as the sociologist Stanley Cohen notes in his detailed study of these seaside clashes, *Folk Devils and Moral Panics*, most of the violence was sporadic and relatively minor when compared to the bloodlettings of the racetrack razor gangs of the 1930s – only two youths were hospitalised with stab wounds over the whole weekend. The one death, reported widely and to maximum effect as 'Mod Dead in Sea' was actually an accident. The youth in question having fallen off the cliffs at Newhaven, seemingly by mistake though suicides were, and continue to be, common enough there. Far from coming tooled up for action, many of the youngsters Cohen himself spoke to in Brighton were woefully unprepared and had only the vaguest ideas about quite why they were there or what they would do. 'Few planned anything,' he wrote, 'they'd expected to find a spot [to sleep] on the beach. Few considered cold weather or rain. Some had come without even a blanket . . . They wandered around rather aimlessly; they were bored and cold.'

TV bulletins from Margate, for all their efforts to create a portrait of a seaside town under siege, tell a similar story. Quizzing a twinkly-eyed old lady with wild grey hair who has just had the glass door of her cafe smashed and was knocked over in an eschewing scrum, one ITN news hound, wheedling for the grisly details, succeeds only in learning that the culprit, a Rocker, was 'such a good looking boy'. And that some of the other Rockers were 'very sweet' and helped her up. He moves on to a trio of Modettes who can scarcely be older than about fifteen, though their deference to him and the guilelessness with which they deal with his questions makes them seem far younger. All of their answers are so redolent of the playground that they could easily be prefaced with the words, 'Please Sir'. Asked who is to blame for the fighting, they respond in unison, 'The Rockers are the ones that do wrong.' Pressed further on this, the girls resort to a kind of they-started-it defence of dinner-queue squabbles, arguing that the Rockers 'get all the Mods into trouble'. Other shots of Rockers, rather geeky-looking types with wonky teeth and in pudding basin-crash helmets leave you wondering just how fearsome any of these youngsters really were. While a claim from one middle-aged holidaymaker, the classic Dad with Brylcreemed hair and in horn-rimmed glasses once to be found on brown sauce bottlenecks and on the sides of model railway kits, that all this violence is the fault of Ban the Bomb marchers, is simply priceless.

The battles would rumble on throughout the rest of that summer, and on into the next, spreading to Hastings, Bournemouth and Southend and becoming, for a short while, a tourist attraction in themselves: a punch-up to view while eating jellied eels instead of some wooden-headed puppets in a booth and an end of pier show. But the shifting tides of fashion and the fickle attention spans of the press soon called time on these coastal jousting matches. In the aftermath of England's World Cup victory in 1966, those looking for a fight gravitated to the football grounds while the arrival of LSD encouraged many Mods and Rockers to embark on rather different kinds of trips.

And if you did still hanker after fresh air, cool water, hot sun, a bag of chips and a likely chance of crumpet, the

Costa Brava rather than Clacton was becoming a far more appealing (and inexpensive) destination. In Margate some forty-five years later, the antics of the Mods and Rockers now seem more like the last great cavort of the English seaside resort, the twitch of a corpse that this generation would now leave for dead.

8

End of the Pierrot

A Pension for Eastbourne – Harold Pinter's
Birthday Party – John le Mesurier sur la Mer –
Washing up with Aleister Crowley – Martin Parr's
Last Resort – Things Have Only Got Better

The sea is grey. A kind of city pigeon grey: a slightly oily looking slate colour, with white and brown flecks that are picked out by what little remains of the late afternoon sun in a cloudy sky. In this light, the pier too appears completely grey. Although its railings are painted a smart royal blue. And most of the Victorian kiosks and turreted booths that cluster along its lengthy deck, rather like the spines on a lizard's back, are white: a colour scheme that recalls football team strips when fans wore home-knitted scarves and carried rattles. And with the whole baroque structure now, at dusk, reduced to a smudgy, ethereal monochrome by an incipient sea mist, the world of Stanley Matthews, coins-in the-meter electricity and lethal smogs could almost never have gone away. It is, however, the sheer numbers of grey and silver-haired people out and about here that helps to confirm that this is the current day. For England has never been more elderly than it is now. The percentage of the population aged over 65 increased by 1.5 million between 1983 and 2008 and the numbers of those aged 85 and over more than doubled to 1.3 million in the same period and are predicted to double again by 2033. Here in Eastbourne, close to a quarter of the population are over 65 while in nearby Rother, the East Sussex administrative district that covers Rye, Battle and Bexhill, that figure reaches a whopping 48.2%.

And where grey waves have long been lapping, more emotive scribes are now writing about an 'age quake' and positing a possible tsunami of elderly people on England's coasts if traditional patterns of migration among retirees continue. It is a big 'if' — research published by Pegasus, the retirement property developers, in November 2009 suggested that there was a subtle shift away from the coast towards inland market towns among newer retirees. And even in Eastbourne, those aged between 25 and 45 currently represent the fastest rising group.

The tradition of seaside retirement is a phenomenon that only dates back to the Edwardian period. By then, as Anthony Hern writes in *The Seaside Holiday*, 'some of the southern resorts had already . . . begun to attract the sort of retired people who were favourite victims of the caricaturists on stage or in the comic papers: Indian Army officers, sea captains, pensioned-off Empire builders.' Their ranks were swelled considerably after the First World War by service veterans, shopkeepers who'd sold out to the new breed of chain stores (the homogenising 'combines' Orwell's George Bowling rails against in *Coming Up for Air*), and professionals realising annuities from investments and/or property. With new bungalows then costing as little as £450, the elderly well could enjoy a comfortable, stair-free dotage by selling up and shifting south. More than one man in ten in Bournemouth, Hastings and Hove gave their occupation as 'retired' in 1931, twice the national average at the time, according to Hern.

Accompanying them in ever greater droves and gaining fast after the Second World War were what might today be called career-shifters or downsizers, those possibly on the cusp of retirement age, opting to leave a prior job or sell their assets to buy a small B&B, a cafe or a gift shop, a deckchair concession, a kiosk on the front, to provide them with a genteel profession and a modest income to ease them through the autumn years.[28] The appeal for both was a supposedly slower pace of life, one dictated by lulling tides and the sense that if everyone is on some sort of holiday or another – and what is retirement, if not a vastly exaggerated, permanently extended vacation? – then the hectic pushes and pulls of ordinary life do not apply. This is the seaside as a waiting-for-god temporal zone where everyone's clock is winding down, and lethargy is seductively contagious and, like salt, hangs thickly in the air all around. Its mood is perhaps never better encapsulated than in *The Birthday Party*, (1958) Harold Pinter's menacing, absurdist comedy set in a seaside boarding house.

Before achieving success as a playwright, Pinter spent about nine years as a jobbing actor in rep, treading the boards in creaky Agatha Christie murder mysteries, Nöel Coward comedies and Ted Willis 'Doctor' farces in such coastal fleapits as the Whitby Spa, Torquay Pavilion, Bournemouth Palace Court and the Worthing Connaught. In the early 1950s and while appearing as Tops in a touring production of L. du Garde Peach's *A Horse! A Horse!*, Pinter was left in Eastbourne without anywhere to stay. Fortunately, he struck up a conversation with a retired concert pianist in a pub. Pitying the young actor's predicament, he invited Pinter back to his own lodgings, and let him have the sofa in his attic room for the week of the play's run.

28 That they might not have had any prior experience in hospitality or retail and that commerce was not the major motivating factor in the establishment of the business, might also help explain the delightful idiosyncrasies of so many seaside guesthouses and shops.

While possibly an improvement on nights under the pier, this accommodation was squalid in the extreme, the sofa shedding hair and dust from the instant Pinter stretched out on it. And then there was the peculiar, not to say queasy, spectacle of the pianist and his landlady. The woman of the house tickling and goosing the musician at every opportunity. In a letter to a friend, Pinter wrote, 'I have filthy insane digs, a great bulging scrag of a woman with breasts rolling at her belly, an obscene household, cats, dogs, tea-strainers, mess, scratch, dung, poison, infantility.' And when he later pressed the pianist on why on earth he remained here, the man could only confess that he had nowhere else to go. From this rather dismal real life scenario, Pinter crafted his first commercially-produced full-length play, with the landlady and the pianist furnishing him with the models for the characters Meg Boles and Stanley Webber.

At the opening of the play, Stanley has all but given up on life. Reeking of decay, he is the archetypal soul adrift, the washed-up creature of the lie-in, the skipped shave and the none-too-clean shirt. The rundown guesthouse he inhabits, if it is a guesthouse (and the issue is left deliberately ambiguous), it soon becomes apparent is metaphorically and, within the context of the drama that unfolds quite literally, purgatory. Goldberg and McCann, the sinister henchmen who arrive to torment the pianist and having broken his will, spirit him away, appear like emissaries from hell. Possibly agents of some totalitarian power, or gangsters – there's a touch of Ronnie and Reggie, down for a couple of days and with people to see, about them – this pair speak in business-y epigrams. Their sentences are peppered with euphemistic allusions to jobs to be done, assignments undertaken and points of procedure. As such it is not too far fetched to see them winding up on some seaside town's council. And possibly less than disinterestedly awarding the building contract for a new marina to a friend of Uncle Barney's.

But by the time Pinter's play was filmed in the late 1960s by the future director of *The Exorcist* William Friedkin and in Worthing, where the dramatist had a *pied a la plage*, the problem of whether to reach out to family holidaymakers or retirees was becoming a far more vexing conundrum for many coastal authorities. There had always been those resorts who'd traded on their gentility and prided themselves on being convivial, quiet retreats for the elderly – Bexhill, Worthing and Eastbourne among them. But with domestic seaside holidays starting to fall off, the likes of Blackpool and others genuinely feared that being lumbered with an ageing contingent of seasonal regulars and older new residents would only further alienate a younger generation of potential visitors. The UK's birth rate reached its all time peak in 1964 – a fact which could well explain why that summer's news was dominated by tales of whipper-snappers running amok on Britain's beaches. With so many babies being born, anyone over thirty could feel positively ancient and, casting around, might also worry that society was spawning a breed of Midwich Cuckoos. But the young had numbers on their side and if seaside towns were to secure any kind of future for themselves, they believed that it made economic sense to doff a kiss-me-quick cap in their direction. The difficulty, however, was that youth culture was more than ever about asserting generational difference through consumer choices and the young didn't necessarily want to do the same things or even inhabit the same physical spaces as their parents or grandparents. Unlike an open to all prom, end of pier show or dance hall, the trendy discotheques and hippie music festivals now springing up policed their doors with the same ageism as the Sandmen in *Logan's Run*. And to be elderly was to be against the grain of those times – rather like old man Steptoe sabotaging poor Harold's ambitions, they were squares bringing the whole scene down, man.

As popular as it was and despite its World War Two setting, the BBC TV comedy *Dad's Army*, entering its opening season as Parisian students were manning the barricades, presented an image of a seaside town as a fogeyish domain of the elderly, the petty and the inept that few then would have wanted to emulate. Here was a southern resort, the fictional Walmington-on-Sea, whose only defence against a possible Nazi invasion was a band of doddery granddads with unreliable bladders led by Captain Mainwaring, a snobbish, martinet bank manager – and native son of Eastbourne – with a distinct inferiority complex and no prior combat experience.

In Sergeant Wilson, played with suave urbanity by John le Mesurier, there was a hint of a man originally destined for better things but, rather like Herman Melville's Bartelby, who'd preferred not to do them. Coasting by on his good looks, easy charm and the kindness of attractive widows, Wilson always surveyed Walmington-on-Sea with the bemusement of one who could never quite work out how he'd ended up there. For the role, Le Mesurier, while very likely channelling a good portion of himself, also seemed to reprise something of an earlier performance as the sand sculptor in Tony Hancock's 1963 film *The Punch and Judy Man*, shot in Bognor Regis.

Carving likenesses of Nelson into the beach at another fictional resort, Piltdown, for indifferent tourists and incontinent dogs, Le Mesurier's Sandman Charles is a similar figure of unfulfilled promise resigned to his fate. Albeit one rather more beaten down by life and unlucky in love than Wilson. This melancholy gentleman artist lives in a beach hut under the pier. On the wall of this wooden shack, where he repairs to brew pots of tea using a special blend of 'Darjeeling with a trace of souchong' that he 'used to have at home' is a framed certificate. Awarded for his art in Cromer in 1935, this memento, like the exotic char, is a symbol of the distinctions of his youth. Their preservation, meanwhile, shows him trying to retain a certain dignity in spite of an obvious fall in circumstances.

Ever since the eighteenth century when the upper classes had used the opportunity to close up their country estates or town houses to live more modestly on the coast, the seaside has always had some associations with slumming it, elegantly or otherwise. Still, until the middle of the twentieth century when they remained synonymous with holidays and therefore a type of leisure previously only available to the affluent, English coastal towns, however tawdry, and tawdriness always has its own special appeal, continued to be held in some esteem. As an escape from the ordinary grind for millions they'd been rendered extraordinary for nearly a century, after all. As daily life became more pleasure orientated for everyone, though, and car ownership, passenger ferries and cheaper flights and so on, encouraged the aspirational to holiday more frequently and further afield, that status went into sharp decline. Post-war suburbanisation had also made some southern coastal towns a lot duller by absorbing them into an expanding commuter belt of dormitory towns.

Patriotic campaigns like 'I'm Backing Britain', launched in 1968 and accompanied by a single by Bruce Forsyth, might have urged consumers to spend those pounds in their pockets on British goods and services. But so many of the finer things in life – Beaujolais Nouveau, Liebfraumilch, Black Forest Gateau, Heineken lager beer, spaghetti bolognese, pizza, fondue – appeared to come from elsewhere. Appearances weren't always everything. But there was an expectation that if you were doing better, you'd be going there too. Perhaps off nibbling a little strudel in a square here, sipping sangria in the sun there and swirling Cognac around enormous vase-size glasses every evening everywhere.[29]

What wasn't all that widely considered, and here there are possibly some loose parallels with the British car industry when consumers started to abandon locally-built

---

29 While hardly a sociological survey but as a litmus test of more general trends, I think it is significant how many episodes of the 1960s BBC sitcom *The Likely Lads* revolve around holidays. In fact, when the viewing public first clapped eyes on Bob and Terry in December 1964, the pair, wearing sombreros and carrying suitcases, were supposedly returning from Spain on their first trip abroad. The difficulty of raising enough funds for a further foreign jaunt provided the plot for one, now lost, episode, entitled 'Faraway Places' and an excursion to a hippy campsite (shades of *Carry on Camping* there) and a boating trip to the Norfolk Broads occur elsewhere. They do not, however, ever visit the seaside, although Scarborough, it emerged in the 1970s sequel *Whatever Happened to the Likely Lads?*, is one of Bob's middle names.

vehicles for cheaper, more reliable foreign models in much the same period, was what long-term effect it would have on the indigenous holiday industry. Good as it might have been for British aviation, the more time and money people spent abroad, the worse things got at home. Previously places where everyone went, seaside towns started to gain a reputation in the national psyche, quite noticeably from the late 1960s onwards, as destinations for people like Pinter's pianist with nowhere better to go or with nothing better to do.

In *The Kindly Ones*, the sixth instalment of Anthony Powell's *A Dance to the Music of Time*, published a little earlier in 1962, the narrator/protagonist, Nicholas Jenkins, is dispatched to the South Coast to clear up his errant Uncle Giles's last effects. The black sheep of the clan, Giles has seen fit to meet his maker on the eve of the Second World War in the Bellevue, a residential hotel of dingy rooms and hard mattresses run by Albert, the Jenkins family's former cook. Serendipitously for the plot and further establishing its déclassé ambience, this seaside dwelling is also home to Bob Dupont, an old acquaintance of Jenkins who is hiding out here from his creditors, and Dr Trelawny, a one-time prominent mystic now a wizened, asthmatic drug addict. As becomes plain when Jenkins and Dupont are called upon to help liberate Trelawny from a hotel bathroom where he's having an asthma attack, the 'athletic, vigorous, prophet of . . . distant days', is in a particularly bad way. Even his beard 'once broad and luxuriant' has shrivelled to a straggly grey goatee 'stained yellow in places'. None too quick in settling his account, in Albert's view, and relying on the 'special pills' that the hotelier perhaps wisely chooses 'not to enquire too closely about' to alleviate the symptoms of his condition, Trelawny is on his last legs. Convinced that the 'climate of this salubrious resort' doesn't really suit him, and only staying on because he 'cannot afford to pay the bill and leave' the Doctor duly exits the Bellevue in much the same manner as Uncle Giles. 'Of course', Albert observes, sanguinely, at one point, 'we have to have all sorts here. We can't pick and choose.' And seaside resorts in general would have to grow far less picky about their clientele in the coming decades.

The character of Trelawny was based on the occultist Aleister Crowley. Dubbed, possibly to his immense satisfaction, 'The Wickedest Man in the World' by the John Bull tattle sheet in 1923, Crowley, much like Trelawny, was to spend his final years hopelessly dependent on heroin and living in a guesthouse by the sea. If similarly penniless and diminished physically by the opiates that were originally prescribed for his asthma, Crowley died in arguably less ignominious circumstances than his fictional counterpart. His last abode, Netherwood in Hastings, a large gabled Victorian mansion (now mostly demolished) standing in four acres of grounds with a shrubbery and a tennis court, positioned in the upland part of the town, was a rather more atypical seaside boarding house than the Bellevue. Though its very atypicality seems typically eccentric and therefore suitably seaside-ish, I suppose. A sign in the hall supposedly outlining the establishment's house rules, gives some understanding of its appeal to Crowley. 'Guests are requested' it stated, 'not to tease the ghosts. Breakfast will be served at 9am to survivors of the night. The Hastings Borough Cemetery is five minutes walk away (ten minutes if carrying body), but only one minute as the Ghost flies. The guests are requested not to cut down bodies from the trees. The Office has a certain amount of used clothing for sale, the property of guests who no longer have any use for earthly raiment.'

Owned and presided over by Vernon Symonds, a gastronome, budding playwright and leading light of the Hastings Court Players dramatic society, and his equally artistically-inclined wife Kathleen (affectionately known as 'Johnny'), Netherwood really aspired to be a salon as much as a guesthouse. Leading public intellectuals of the day such as BBC radio's *The Brains Trust* panel member and, later, convicted rail fare dodger, C.E.M. Joad, were invited to stay there free of charge in exchange for giving a talk on a topic of interest and leading discussions over supper. And a young Julian Bream was among the musicians who gave recitals in its dinning room.

Moving into Room 13 at the front of the building shortly before his seventieth birthday in early September 1945, the self-styled Great Beast 666 proved an agreeable and well-liked member of the household. Whether chatting animatedly with his hosts and the other residents, taking a regular morning constitutional around the grounds, snacking on sardines sprinkled with curry powder in his room or besting opponents at the Hasting Chess Club, of which he became the reigning and undefeated grand master, Crowley cut a rather avuncular, not to say grandfatherly figure. Only the occasional visit from the odd still-loyal disciple and a nocturnal regimen devoted to reading arcane texts, writing letters, chanting spells and injecting the junk that arrived in rations from Heppel's the chemist in London, gave any serious indication of an earlier life spent as the scourge of western civilization. Leaving this dimension on 1 December 1947 after a bout of pneumonia, Crowley came to an earthly end in a part of Hastings that rises far above a local district called Bohemia. The symbolism, you suspect, would not have been lost on the Satanist himself.

'Do what thou wilt shall be the whole of the law' was one of Crowley's most infamous pronouncements. One that was embraced in spirit and with occasionally catastrophic results some two decades after his death by a new generation who were sampling drugs, free love and esoteric religions for themselves. Though the Summer of Love was to be brief and its ideals all but frozen out by the Winter of Discontent, the long-term consequences of this pivotal period of sexual and narcotic experimentation were to be as keenly felt on the coasts as anywhere else in Britain. As a pensioner and a drug user, Crowley was in many respects highly emblematic of the two groups that would come to dominate any discussion of seaside towns in the fading years of the twentieth century.

Though heroin, cocaine and cannabis were popular among the monde and demi-monde in the 1920s and 30s, recreational drug use remained extremely rare in Britain until the late 1950s. The majority of fully fledged addicts in the country before that were, like Crowley, elderly and had acquired their habit through some kind of medical treatment. Only 1,053 heroin addicts were 'known to the Home Office' in 1967 – in 1955 there had been just 47. (Current estimates by the Joseph Rowntree Trust put the numbers of 'problem heroin users' at about 200,000.) Until 1968, when tougher restrictions were enacted, scripts of the drug could still be obtained from a sympathetic doctor, if one could be found. In fact, the new legislation had largely been passed because a small group of medics were believed to be fuelling a rapidly growing black market in the drug among London's youth by over-prescribing. Two of the most notorious offenders were Lady Isabella Frankau who before her death in 1967 ran an up-market psychiatric practice in Wimpole Street and was alleged to have signed out over 600,000 tablets of heroin in 1962 alone, and Dr John Petro. Subsequently vilified as 'the junkie's friend' by the press when he was arrested and struck off in 1968, Petro operated in far less prestigious surroundings. Having lost his own practice through bankruptcy but not his licence, he set up shop outside the all-night Boots chemist at Piccadilly Circus and in various hotels, pubs and underground stations and sold prescriptions at £3 a pop to all comers.

However, given a back-story of dubious quackery, maritime trade in opium and as the easiest entry point for just about all and any contraband or proscribed goods into the country, narcotics have, of course, always been taken at the seaside. We only have to look back to *Evil Under the Sun* and Agatha Christie to unearth, an admittedly fictional, case of heroin trafficking at a coastal resort.

In this 1941 novel, Horace Blatt, a parvenu guest at the exclusive Jolly Roger Hotel on Smuggler's Island (cue orchestra with suspenseful sounding 'dum dum . . . daaah' chords) off the Devon coast is 'banged to rights' as a drug runner. A store of dark green tin picnic boxes ingeniously marked 'sandwiches', 'salt', 'pepper' and 'mustard' to avert suspicion but actually filled with diamorphine hydrochloride are unearthed near his yacht in Pixy Cove. 'This isn't salt, sir. Not by a long way! Bitter taste! Seems to me it's some kind of drug', Sergeant Phillips, displaying a knowledge of pharmacology far beyond the ken of most coppers in Christie mysteries, tells his superior, Inspector Colgate, as they paw the illicit booty.

As areas with floating populations of visiting urban pleasure-seekers, seasonal employment and (due to the high numbers of retirees) plenty of burglar-able pharmacies, the larger seaside towns were – and remain – as good a place as any in England to score and do drugs.[30]

In the late 1960s, Brighton was one of the first places to acquire a drug-dependency unit, evidence that addiction was already starting to be recognised as an issue there. Though in an era when few such clinics existed, it probably had the added, if unintended consequence, of attracting users who wanted to get straight into the area. (And, also, perhaps, interdependently increasing the number of dealers who knew there was a captive audience, too.)

There was at this stage, it should be remembered, an enormous amount of naivety about drugs, which continued to be a novelty. Like sex then, and pre-AIDS, drugs were still rather shocking, and, consequently, in some quarters, seen

---

30) While sentencing a former wrench monkey for dealing heroin and crack cocaine in June 2007, Judge Richard Hayward had happened to remark to the jury at Hove Crown Court that 'it was easier to buy drugs than it was to get a plumber in Hastings'. The local paper, the *Argus*, decided to put the judge's claims to the test. Reporter Andy Whelan called ten plumbers in the Hastings area asking for someone to fix a leaky tap. He received no reply from five, 'three said they could come within three hours while one said tomorrow and another next week'. Heading down to the seafront, however, he met a group of young men, and within 53 minutes had secured 'a couple of grammes of cocaine and an eighth of an ounce of grass'.

as naughty but nice. Both those who touted their pleasures and consciousness-raising possibilities and those who dismissed them out of hand were prone to exaggeration. The latter falling too easily into horror stories and simplistic moral condemnations. And the former, romanticising even wanton self-destruction, and tending to believe that their ingestion was paving the way for a social or spiritual revolution. The result in the late 1960s, however, was that rising consumption was met with ever more draconian legislation. This did little to stem demand. In trying to restrict supply it arguably only further helped to encourage their trade by making drugs a more profitable criminal commodity. (And from hereon in drugs were certainly a commodity that professional criminals took a much more diligent, not to say, proprietorial, interest in.)

Turning again to fiction, and once more to *The History Man*, Malcolm Bradbury's novel offers a near contemporary snapshot of a coastal university town, loosely styled after Brighton, that provides almost in passing a glimpse of that period's druggy, slightly damaged, milieu. The book's protagonists, the radical sociology lecturer Howard Kirk and his wife Barbara, arrive in 'Watermouth' from Leeds in the autumn of 1967. Initially the Kirks are worried that their new southern home with its funfair, old private hotels and new flatlets is too bourgeois. But they are soon shown the urban blight lurking behind the 'holiday facade' by Ella, an ex-student from Leeds now working in the local Social Security department. Watermouth, she reassures them 'is a problem town'. 'It's full of hippies and dropouts. All these places are. It's a town you can run to and disappear. There are empty houses. Visitors are soft touches. Lots of marginal work.' And any lingering doubts are finally banished when Ella leads the Kirks on a tour of a condemned property, all broken banisters, smashed glass and piles of human shit, where meth drinkers, junk fiends and teenage runaways all apparently kip. As pictures of dereliction go it could, of course, be almost anywhere in Britain and at almost any time between the 1960s and today – though meths in a world where a can of 'vandal-strength lager' is cheaper than a cup of tea is something that even the 'wankers on the street' can avoid nowadays. (Who knows, though – with plans to introduce unit per alcohol pricing on the cards, it could easily be back 'on trend' for tramps again soon . . . Tuborg lager, ballroom dancing, and even the seaside, have after all already been rehabilitated . . .) As an already retrospective glimpse of the wasted getting wasted on the coast, however, it actually seems an eerily far-sighted portrait, if anything, of the 1980s and 90s.

Bradbury was apparently rather unhappy that after his novel was adapted for television and broadcast in 1981, it was taken in some quarters as an endorsement of Thatcherism. Naturally, he had the last laugh in 1987 with *Cuts*, a satirical romp through 80s Britain, a period, in his view, when the 'old soft illusions' were busily being replaced 'with the new hard illusions'. But the winners and the losers of the Conservative government's policies and a banking-led, post-industrial economy were not too difficult to spot beside the sea, the distinctions between the two growing ever more pronounced.

Jonathan Raban, sailing round the country at the time of the Falklands War for his book *Coasting*, was able to note a conspicuous number of shiny new yachts and folksy but expensive cafes, art galleries and antique shops in places like Rye. It is revealing that when the BBC were looking for a homegrown drama that would capture the zeitgeist – and zeitgeist was quite the phrase of this supposedly whizzily, entrepreneurial period – in the manner of a US show like *Dynasty*, it commissioned *Howards' Way*, the everyday story of Hampshire marina folk who built fibreglass catamarans and ran fashion houses, drank spritzers and wore pastel knitwear. Though if anything, much of the terrain had already been scoped out by *Bergerac*. This Jersey-set detective series starring John Nettles ran from 1981 until 1991, the year Thatcher herself was forced from office. And in presenting an idealised version of what living on an island with low taxation, thriving service industries, a population of millionaires, strict rules on residency, vintage cars and where most crimes seemed to involve some kind of connection to France (for which read Europe, at large), it was the Tory dream of England in microcosm.

At the other end of the scale and the country were Martin Parr's rather pitiless photographs of New Brighton. Using bright, saturated full-English breakfast colour and homing his lens on the holidaymakers at this seaside resort just outside Liverpool, he created an almost Bosch-ian portrait of degradation. Though light on trepanning, here was a hell where screaming kids and their dead-eyed parents sat beside piles of litter, eating disgustingly greasy food on a waterfront so scummy and polluted it looked like the worm-infested garbage pool in *Star Wars*.

Exhibited under the title 'The Last Resort' at the Serpentine Gallery in 1986, Parr's show was condemned by some critics for stripping his subjects of their dignity for the amusement of sophisticated art-goers. Empathy might have been thinner on the ground than some might have liked, and exaggeration part of the game. But shot when the loss of manufacturing jobs and the decline of the docks meant unemployment was running at 25% in Liverpool and in some parts of the city there was close to 90% youth unemployment, and soon to be awash with cheap brown heroin, it was as honest a depiction of the plight of the working classes under Thatcher as anything else. There was nothing especially romantic about what they were trying to make do with at the time.

In 1969 what remained of the buildings of the New Brighton Tower, on its completion in 1900 the highest building in the country, had burnt to the ground, leaving behind a derelict wasteland. Just under a decade later its Promenade pier had been dismantled and changes in tidal conditions in the River Mersey had eroded the beach's sands to such an extent that all that was left was a shelf of rock and stone. And the indignities continued after Parr's exhibition; in 1990 its champion-sized swimming stadium, a Deco masterpiece in Snowcrete, caved in during a severe storm and, lacking the estimated £4 million needed to repair it, the Merseyside Development Corporation levelled the site with bulldozers.

The pool had hosted the Miss New Brighton bathing beauty contest for the previous, consecutive forty-nine years. At the competition's debut in 1949, some 15,000 people had paid to marvel at the spectacle. This sort of gigantism was – and is – at the heart of the problems many seaside towns have faced since the 1960s. Laid out in the nineteenthth century and expanded in the early twentieth, they'd been built to handle a huge volume of holidaymakers. In 1938, when the national population stood at about 46 million, some 7 million people were reputed to have visited Blackpool, which was then able 'to accommodate half a million in a single night'. Southend was calculated to attract some 5.5 million visitors, 'four-fifths of them between Whitsun and the end of September', while nearly 3 million made it to Hastings, 2 million hit Bournemouth and Southport, and even Ramsgate and Eastbourne got over a million each.

Most of those visits, as the figures for Southend suggest, would have been undertaken during the summer season. This brought great clusters of sun-and-sand seekers to the coasts over relatively brief periods with the predictability of the tides. Once those patterns began to change, however, almost all seaside resorts were left with a vast surplus of capacity. And, equally, of course, a range of amenities that an increasing number of the population regarded as old hat if not plain naff when placed beside newer safari parks, water worlds and living museums – to say nothing of what could be enjoyed on an overseas package deal or a trekking break in India, say.

Accordingly, hotels with empty guest books were converted into retirement flats and nursing homes or knocked down to make way for new shopping malls in the hope of cresting on the retail wave. But as the 1980s tipped into the 1990s and the economy, almost from the instant Gazza burst into tears, went into freefall, those shops were left empty and spare seaside accommodation was used to provide most-needed emergency housing for the homeless and asylum seekers fleeing the various ethnic conflicts that had sprung up since the collapse of the Soviet Union.

Even after the downturn had ended, the recession of the early 1990s was to leave many British resorts deeply scarred. As cash-strapped local councils and private landlords had scrimped on repairs or indulged in bouts of fund-liquidating sprees of arson (not the councils, obviously, perish the thought), many cut a less than edifying jib. Folkestone, once 'the gem of the Kentish coast' was granted 'assisted-area status' in the 1990s. Nearly a decade after Norman Lamont was wibbling on about 'the green shoots of recovery', the buildings of one of its most illustrious seafront crescents still lay empty and their windows filled in with breeze-blocks. While a quarter of Rhyl's population, (technically outside this book's stated jurisdiction), were reported to be 'living in long-term bed and breakfast accommodation'. In 1996 it was christened the 'Costa del Dole' and rated 'Britain's least sexy holiday spot' in one poll. And the BBC was reporting 'a heroin crisis' in Brighton two years later and the *Guardian* a narcotic-related 'Tide of Misery' in Great Yarmouth.

From here things could, to paraphrase a song popular at the time, really only get better. For some anyway. Although the New Labour government that assumed power in 1997 at the height of Cool Britannia and the Young British Artists, when Union Jacks and beach huts alike were revived with a veneer of knowing irony, remained committed, at least according to Philip Gould, to fulfilling 'ordinary people's' aspirations 'to go on holiday in Spain rather than Bournemouth'. A steady economy, a housing boom, the high rate of the pound and the arrival of budget airlines

– and Ryanair and EasyJet still ferried some 65.3 and 46.1 million passengers across Europe, respectively, in staycation 2009 – were, in any case, to ensure that cheap foreign travel became a banal fact of life, little more taxing than sending an email halfway around the world, during most of the opening decade of the new century.

But in the same period, a growing awareness of the environmental cost of air travel and, perhaps, a sense that jetting off here, there and everywhere of a weekend was so easy and inexpensive that it had ceased to be special and had become instead rather vulgar, was also to cause many people to reassess the idea of holidaying at home. (Holidaying at home, at a time when credit was plentiful, itself just another or many options.)

To begin with it was second-home spots, of which there were now more than ever, in Devon, Cornwall or Suffolk or broadsheet-anointed bolt holes from the capital such as Brighton, Broadstairs and Whitstable that flourished. Though the Rabelaisian qualities of a stag-do in Blackpool were from time to time hymned. Economic confidence breeding a kind of confidence about what had once been regarded as parochial and provincial. But with so many of the neglected districts or abandoned industrial spaces of inner urban centres homogenised and expensified, there had been more general relocation by the property-hungry, the impecunious, the artistic and the curious, to the remoter aquatic peripheries of the land. Bohemia would once again be sought in Bohemia, East Sussex.

This pattern of reclaiming – if possibly, in the process subsequently taming – the obsolescent and the neglected has been the abiding story of the previous two (or even now, three) decades' gentrification, the nation's last great game. Where those in pursuit of the edgy and the unclaimed seized possibilities in the centre, now only the edges remain. What was once limiting about seaside towns, their remoteness and melancholy ruination, when cities were still limitless and full of nooks and crannies to be colonised and quarried, is proving to be their salvation.

The seaside, though, was always about being somewhere else, in English life. Historically, literally points of departure for travellers, its stock in trade was offering a departure from normality. The architecture, from the ornamental iron balustrades and Raj bandstands to the glitterball-lit ballrooms and neon-signed amusement arcades, seduced by transporting visitors into realms of fantasy. The sea itself a reminder that here in England, the world really was at your feet, if you were willing to take the plunge.

Stepping away from this for a few moments to make a cup of coffee, I started flipping idly through a Sunday broadsheet's magazine and found myself reading a review of a restaurant in Ramsgate. Were there reviews of restaurants in Ramsgate ten years ago? Did I even bother to look at restaurant reviews ten years ago? Is it the age? Or my age? In either case, the tide has definitely turned.

Epilogue

The thing about the movie *Quadrophenia*, as anyone will tell you, is that it begins at the end.

The film's opening minutes are taken up with Phil Daniels as the Mod Jimmy on a beach. He emerges as if from the ocean. And looking not unlike a turtle, since he is wearing an oversized green parka with sleeves that obscure his hands. Scuttling away from the foreshore, fists encased in canvas, he grows to fill up the screen. Daniels moves determinedly, if rather unsteadily, and zigzagging slightly. His head bobs up and down as he powers toward the viewer. The cloth of his straight-legged trousers flaps, their immaculate lines spoiled by his overeager motions. The hem of that parka, in turn, beats out a tattoo on his knees. All the while, crashing waves and snatches of Roger Daltrey's voice, phased and drenched in echo, slosh around, providing a kind of aural amniotic to the events at hand. And the whole scene does have a peculiarly womb-like quality, bathed as it is in a Belisha beacon orange glow from a setting (or possibly rising) sun. A sun that soon enough morphs into a scooter headlight and begins a less than celestial orbit of the Goldhawk Road, whizzing past Triumph 1100s and MGBs – visitors themselves from a near future in the movie's 1964 time frame. But just before that, it is the loping figure of Daniels that commands attention, alone. His pale face (possibly bloodied and rather vole-like) and his eyes (deep set and noticcably glassy) are illuminated for a second or two as he ducks right and the screen is overcome by that scooter-light sun. In those brief few moments, a grim commitment to life and away from the sea, it subsequently becomes apparent, has been made.

We go on to see Jimmy become enchanted by Brighton during a weekend of revelry that includes some action in an alley with Leslie Ash. Back in town, life isn't the same. '[N]othing seems right, apart from Brighton' he complains at one point, before deciding to head back to the coast, only to be bitterly disappointed by what he finds there this time. He has made that most classic of errors: mistaking a holiday for ordinary life. And like a pebble that looks so shiny on the shore but at home appears merely dull, perhaps the true magic of the seaside is that its pleasures are individual, fleeting and wrapped up in the whole.

Acknowledgements

Thanks are first due to everyone at Sceptre and Hodder but in particular to Jocasta Hamilton and Helen Coyle. It was Helen who first suggest that I 'should write something about the seaside'. And this rather wayward book is that 'something'.

My agent Nicola Barr's support, wise council and kind words were invaluable throughout.

I am immensely grateful to the staff at the British Library in St Pancras and in Colindale and The London Library in St James's who kept me supplied with books, newspapers and provided Wi-Fi friendly googling environments to plan various trips around the coast. To that end I'd like to thank Eugene Wolstenholme for being 'my native companion' on jaunts to Blackpool, New Brighton and Southport, Andy Miller for the low-down on Whitstable, Eithne Farry for advice on Broadstairs and Thanet, Andrew Martin for words of wisdom about Scarborough, Steve Fagan and the Squadron Leaders for surf music in Brighton and Andy King for sharing his memories of working at Butlin's Skegness, Alice Maddicott for many thoughts on the wayoutness of the west and Frances Morgan for her eloquent advocacy of the watery bits of Essex. And Konrad Fredericks, a true puppet master, for explaining the art of Mr Punch.

Simon Grant of TATE ETC., and Picpus and Guy Sangster-Adams of *Plectrum* magazine kindly provided me with opportunities to write about things coastal related.

Alex Major perhaps even more kindly read a draft of the book and provided many useful suggestions.

And now I must just resort (no pun intended) to a list of friends, colleagues and souls who have been nice along the way and seek forgiveness from anyone I have inadvertently forgotten, so thank you: Lauren Wright, Gail O'Hara, Richard Boon, Bob Stanley, Ben Thompson, Barney Hoskyns, Mick Brown, Sukhdev Sandu, Ian Sansom, Steve Jelbert, Dan Carrier, Andrew Holgate, John Doran, Chris Roberts, Declan Clarke, Rachel Bailey, Essie Cousins, Angela Penhaligon, Gwendolen MacKeith, Ralf Obergfell, Catherine Taylor, Katrina Dixon, Michael Knight, Simon Hughes, Hannah Connelly, John Noi, Dusty Miller, Bruno Vincent, Louise Campbell, Ashley Biles, Nick Rennison, Nick Tucker, Nick Parker, Karen Mcleod, Henry Jeffreys, Paula Byerly Croxon, Sarah Maguire, Deborah Bourne, Tom Boll, Charles Beckett, Julia Bird, David 'Emit Bloch' Turin, Kate Pemberton, Martin and Judy Bax, Geoff Nicholson, Helen Gordon, Emily Berry, Mike Smith, Tom Chivers, Sam Hawkins and Marie McPartin, Amy Prior, Anna Goodall and Tim Wells, Richard Thomas and John Williams, Dotun Adebayo and Sophia Dettmer, Joe Kerr, Jason Shelley, John Grindrod, Gerry Hopkinson, Victoria Jane Mitchinson, Nikesh Shukla, Lyn and the Haggle Records team, Raz at the Betsy Trotwood, everyone at the London Transport Museum, Snappy Snaps Islington, Richard Nash and Carrie Dieringer.

Which leaves space, just about, to thank, my folks without whom . . . and, my wife, Emily Bick, whose brilliant mind and astonishing beauty I am blessed with every day.

Sources

Rather like a holiday scrapbook, full of ticket stubs, hotel match-books, newspaper clippings, bits of shell, dried seaweed, sun cream stained postcards and slightly out of focus photographs, this book owes a huge debt to numerous earlier seaside histories, guidebooks and articles. The sources and select bibliography below should hopefully give credit where credit is due and point those who want to know more in the right directions.

Introduction

Bill Cormack's *A History of Holidays: 1812–1990* (London: Routledge/Thoemmes, 1998).

The Idler Book of Crap Towns: The 50 Worst Places to Live in the UK, ed. Sam Jordison and Dan Kieran (London: Boxtree, 2003).

Heinz's lines were lifted from *Telstar: The Joe Meek Story* (2008), scripted by James Hicks and Nick Moran.

All the material on the Festival of Britain is taken from *The South Bank Exhibition: A Guide to the Story it Tells*, Ian Cox (London: 1951).

Betjeman's Margate, 1940 can be found in *Collected Poems*, New Edition (London: John Murray, 2006).

Wish You Were Here (1987) was written and directed by David Leland. The current DVD version produced by Cinema Club 2001, includes an illuminating interview with Leland.

For the sale of Emin's beach hut installation 'The Last Thing I Said To You Is Don't Leave Me Here', see 'Tracey Emin enters her blue beach hut period', Nigel Reynolds, *Daily Telegraph*, 13 September 2000.

For the reports by the TUC and the Centre for Cities on rising unemployment is seaside towns see 'How is Britain coping with the recession? – Hastings', Samira Shackle, *New Statesman*, 10 September 2009 and BBC News website 'Unemployment hits seaside resorts', 21 August 2009.

See 'Seaside towns' rising tide of personal insolvencies', Elizabeth Judge, *The Times*, 26 October 2009 for bankruptcies.

Chapter One: Half in Love with Easeful Death

For the transformation of the sea from a monster into the thing of health giving sublimity and much else throughout the book see: *The Englishman's Holiday: A Social History*, J. R. Pimlott (London: Faber, 1947), *Seaside England*, Ruth Manning-Sanders (London: Batsford, 1951), *The Seaside Holiday: The History of the English Seaside Resort*, Anthony Hern (London: The Cresset Press, 1967), *The English Seaside*, H. G. Stokes (London: Sylvan Press, 1947), *Beside the Seaside,* James Walvin (London: Penguin, 1978), *The Beach: The History of Paradise on Earth*, Lena Lenek and Gideon Bosker (London: Secker & Warburg, 1998), *The Seaside, Health and the Environment in England and Wales Since 1800*, John Hassan (Ashgate Aldershot: Burlington, 2003), *The English Spa: 1560–1815*, Phyliss Hembry (London: The Athlone Press, 1980), and John Travis 'Continuity and Change in English Sea-Bathing,

1730–1900' in *Recreation and the Sea*, ed. Stephen Fisher (Exeter: University of Exeter Press, 1997).

For more on Richard Russell and Brighton see *The Man Who Invented the Seaside*, Jean Garratt (Brighton: Royal Pavilion, Art Gallery and Museums, 1977).

Quotes from Addison and Burke's are taken from their appearances in *The Oxford Book of the Sea*, ed. Jonathan Raban (Oxford: Oxford University Press, 1992), which was equally indispensable to rest of this chapter.

Defoe's description of Brighton is from A Tour Through the Whole Island of Great Britain, abridged and edited with an introduction and notes by Pat Rogers (London: Penguin, 1979).

Quotes from Margaret Drabble are from *A Writer's Britain: Landscape in Literature* (London: Thames and Hudson, 1979).

Quotes from Austen's Sanditon were from *Northanger Abbey; Lady Susan; The Watsons; and Sanditon,* Jane Austen; edited by John Davie (Oxford: Oxford University Press, 1980). For background see: *Jane Austen: The World of Her Novels*, Deirdre Le Faye (London: Frances Lincoln, 2002), *Life in Regency England*, RJ White (London: Batsford, 1963) and *Jane Austen and Representations of Regency England*, Roger Sales (London: Routledge, 1994).

For the medical treatments of the period see: *Blood and Guts,* Roy Porter (London: Allen Lane, 2002) and *Gout: The Patrician Malady,* Roy Porter and G.S. Rousseau (New Haven/London: Yale University Press, 1998).

For the specific ailments of the Hanoverians see: *Purple Secret: Genes, 'Madness' and the Royal Houses of Europe,* Rohl,

Warren and Hunt (London: Corgi Books, 1999), *George III and the Mad-Business*, Ida Macalpine and Richard Hunter (London: Pimlico, 1991), *Madmen: A Social History of Madhouses, Mad Doctors & Lunatics*, Roy Porter (Stroud: Tempus, 2004), *George III: A Personal History*, Christopher Hibbert (London: Viking, 1998), *George IV: Prince of Wales 1762–1811*, Christopher Hibbert (London: Longman, 1972) and *Our Tempestuous Day: A History of Regency England*, Carolly Erickson (London: Robson Books, 1996).

For Lady Marlborough's description of seabathing in Scarborough see: *Letter of a Grandmother, 1732–1735, Being the Correspondence of Sarah, Duchess of Marlborough with her Granddaughter Diana, Duchess of Bedford*, ed. Gladys Scott Thomson (London: Jonathan Cape, 1943).

The review of Sheridan's Scarborough Spa is quoted in *The Life and Works of Sheridan*, James Morwood (Edinburgh: Scottish Academic Press, 1985).

For the early years of Scarborough see: *A Guide to Historic Scarborough*, Scarborough Archaeological and Historical Society (Stockton on Tees: Falcon Press, 2003)

For the Brontës see: *The Life of Charlotte Brontë*, Elizabeth Gaskell; edited with an introduction and notes by Angus Eason (Oxford: Oxford University Press, 1996) *The Brontë Letters* selected and with an introduction by Muriel Spark (London: Nevill, 1954) *The Brontë Myth*, Lucasta Miller (London: Jonathan Cape, 2001) *The Brontës By the Sea: An account of Charlotte and Anne Brontë's visits to the East and North Yorkshire coast of England*, Rhonda Petersen (Bridlington: Bretlington Publishing, 1997).

Chapter Two: Sex on the Beach

For mass observation material on the sexual antics of seaside resorts (or lack of them) see *Worktowners at Blackpool: Mass-Observation and Popular Leisure in the 1930s*, ed. Gary Cross (London: Routledge 1990).

Stanley Houghton's 1912 play *Hindle Wakes* to date has been filmed four times, twice silent, in 1918 and 1927 (both directed by Maurice Elvey), and twice again with sound, in 1931 and 1952. The description of the signing of the register is taken from the 1952 version directed by Arthur Crabtree.

George Harvey Bone is the protagonist of *Hangover Square: A Story of Darkest Earl's Court*, Patrick Hamilton; with an introduction by J.B. Priestley, (London: Penguin, 2001, c1941).

And T. S. Eliot's The Waste Land is in *Collected Poems 1909–62* (London: Faber new edition, 2002).

For Donald McGill see George Orwell 'The Art of Donald McGill' and *Wish You Were Here: The Art of Donald McGill* Arthur Calder Marshall, (London: Hutchinson, 1966).

For Alain Corbin's sexualized reading of the beach see *The Lure of the Sea: The Discovery of the Seaside in the Western World, 1750–1840*, Alain Corbin; translated by Jocelyn Phelps (Cambridge: Polity, 1994).

For the Prince Regent see *George III: A Personal History* Christopher Hibbert, (London: Viking, 1998), *George IV: Prince of Wales 1762–1811*, Christopher Hibbert (London: Longman, 1972), and *George IV, Regent and King, 1811–1830* (London: Allen Lane, 1973), plus *Our Tempestuous Day: A History of Regency England*, Carolly Erickson (Robson Books: London, 1996), *Life in Regency England*, RJ White (London: Batsford,

1963) and *The Disastrous Marriage: A Study of George IV and Caroline of Brunswick*, Joanna Richardson (Westport, Conn.: Greenwood Press, 1975).

For Mrs Creevey's account of a night in the Pavilion see *Thomas Creevey's Papers*, selected and edited by John Gore (Harmondsworth: Penguin, 1985, c1948).

For the early years of Brighton see the general seaside histories per Chapter One and *Brighton, Old Ocean's Bauble*, Edmund William Gilbert (Hassocks: Flare Books, 1975), *Life in Brighton: from the earliest times to the present*, Clifford Mugrave (London: Faber, 1970), *The Pictorial History of Brighton and the Royal Pavilion*, Clifford Mugrave (London: Pitkin Pictorials, 1959), *The making of the Royal Pavilion, Brighton: designs and drawings*, John Morley (London: Philip Wilson, 2003), *A history of the Royal Pavilion, Brighton: with an account of its original furniture and decoration*, Henry David Roberts (London: Country Life, 1939) and again for Russell, *The Man Who Invented the Seaside*, Jean Garratt (Brighton: Royal Pavilion, Art Gallery and Museums, 1977).

Also see *Made in Brighton: From the Grand to the Gutter-Modern Britain as Seen from Beside the Sea*, Julie Burchill and Daniel Raven (London: Virgin, 2007) for much on the seamier side of Brighton including the account of George Wilson's attempt to persuade a guardsman to commit an unnatural act in 1822.

Chapter Three: We Are Not Amused

For the birth of the railways see: *The Railways of Britain*, Jack Simmons (London: Macmillan, 1986), *Victorian Railway*, Jack Simmons (London: Thames & Hudson, 1995), *The Victorian Railway and How It Evolved*, P. J. G. Ransom (London: William Heinemann, 1990) and *Fire & Steam: A New History of the Railways in Britain*, Christian Wolmar (London: Atlantic, 2007).

For the piers see: *Pavilions on the Sea: A History of the Seaside Pier*, Cyril Bainbridge (London: Hale, 1986), *British Seaside Piers*, Chris Mawson and Richard Riding (Hersham: Ian Allan, 2008), *Piers and other Seaside Architecture*, Lynn F. Pearson (Princes Risborough: Shire, 2008), *British Piers*, photographs by Richard Fischer; introduction by John Walton (London: Thames & Hudson, 1987) and *Walking Over the Waves: Quintessential British Seaside Piers*, Chris Foote Wood (Dunbeath: Whittles, c2008) and *The Brighton Chain Pier: In memoriam, its history from 1823 to 1896, with a biographical notice of Sir Samuel Brown, its designer and constructor, etc.* (Brighton: J. G. Bishop, 1896) and *Brighton's West Pier*, Peter E.W. Best (Brighton: Brighton Society, 1974) and *Walking on Water: The West Pier Story*, Fred Gray; foreword by Asa Briggs (Brighton: Brighton West Pier Trust, 1998).

For the Great Exhibition see: *The Great Exhibition of 1851: A Nation on Display*, Jeffrey A. Auerbach (New Haven, CT: Yale University Press, 1999), *The World for a Shilling: How the Great Exhibition of 1851 Shaped a Nation*, Michael Leapman (London: Headline, 2001) and *The Victorians*, A.N. Wilson (London: Hutchinson, 2002) – which also inspired much else in this chapter.

For Thomas Cook and Bank Holidays see *The Business of Travel: A Fifty Years' Record of Progress*, W. Fraser Rae (London: Thos. Cook & Son 1891), *The Thomas Cook Story*, John Pudney, (London: Michael Joseph, 1953), *The Romantic Journey: the Story of Thomas Cook and Victorian Travel*, Edward Swinglehurst (London: Pica Editions, 1974) and *Thomas Cook: 150 years of Popular Tourism*, Piers Brendon (London: Secker & Warburg, 1991).

For the Tuggs family see *Sketches by Boz*, Charles Dickens; edited with an introduction and notes by Dennis Walder and original illustrations by George Cruikshank (London: Penguin, 1995) and for Pooter in Broadstairs see *The Diary of a Nobody,* George and Weedon Grossmith with illustrations by Weedon Grossmith (Harmondsworth: Penguin, 1979).

For Gosse and the vogue for exploring rock pools see *Sea-Side Pleasures,* Philip Henry Gosse and Emily Gosse (London: S.P.C.K, 1853), *Father and Son: A Study of Two Temperaments*, Edmund Gosse (Harmondsworth: Penguin Books, 1970) and *Glimpses of the Wonderful: The Life of Philip Henry Gosse, 1810–1888*, Ann Thwaite (London: Faber, 2002).

Quotes from *The French Lieutenant's Woman* are John Fowles (London: Cape, 1969).

For minstrels and pierrots see *Blacking up: The Minstrel Show in Nineteenth Century America,* Robert C. Toll (New York: Oxford University Press, 1974) and 'The Banjo in Britain' , W. M. Brewer, BMG magazine, December 1955.

For fish and chips see *Fish and Chips and the British Working Class, 1870–1940,* John K. Walton (Leicester University Press, 1992).

For ice cream see *Harvest of the Cold Months: The Social History of Ice and Ices,* Elizabeth David, edited by Jill Norman (London: M. Joseph,1994), *A History of the British Ice Cream Industry,* Basil Crowhurst (Westerham: Food Trade, 2000) and *Licks, Sticks & Bricks: A World History of Ice Cream,* Pim Reinders (Rotterdam: Unilever, 1999).

For Punch and Judy see *Punch & Judy: A History,* George Speaight (London: Studio Vista, 1970), *Punch and Judy: Its Origin and Evolution,* Michael Byrom (Norwich: DaSilva Puppet Books, 1988) and, in particular, Philip John Stead's *Mr Punch,* (London: Evans Bros, 1950).

For Blackpool see general seaside histories from Chapter One and James Laver in *Beside the Sea,* ed. Yvonne Cloud (London: Stanley Nott, 1934), *A Century of Fun,* Peter Bennett (Blackpool: Blackpool Pleasure Beach, 1996), *Blackpool,* John K. Walton (Carnegie Publishing, 1998) along with Walton's *The Blackpool Landlady: A Social History* (Manchester: Manchester University Press, 1978) and his *Riding on Rainbows: Blackpool Pleasure Beach and Its Place in British Popular Culture* (St Albans: Skelter, 2007).

For Esme Collings and birth of British film see *Who's Who of Victorian Cinema: A Worldwide Survey* edited by Stephen Herbert and Luke McKernan (London: British Film Institute, 1996), *Pioneers of the British film, Vol. 3, 1898: The Rise of the Photoplay,* John Barnes (London: Bishopsgate Press, 1983) and *Shepperton Babylon: The Lost Worlds of British Cinema,* Matthew Sweet (London: Faber and Faber, 2005).

For an impressionistic snapshot of the seaside at the outbreak of the First World War see *Before the Lamps Went Out,* Geoffrey Marcus (London: Allen and Unwin, 1965).

Chapter Four: Thoroughly Moderne

George Orwell's essay on crime fiction is the title essay in *Decline of the English Murder and other Essays* (Harmondsworth: Penguin, 1965).

Quotes from *Evil Under the Sun* are Agatha Christie (London: HarperCollins, 1999, c1941).

For Agatha Christie and her world see *Agatha Christie: An Autobiography* (Collins: London, 1977), *Agatha Christie: A Biography* Janet Morgan (London: Fontana, 1985), *The Agatha Christie Companion: The Complete*

Guide to Agatha Christie's Life and Work, Dennis Sanders and Len Lovallo, (New York: Delacorte Press, 1984), *The Getaway Guide to Agatha Christie's England*, Judith Diana Hurdle (Oakland, Calif: RDR Books, 1999) and Colin Watson's superb and magnificently irreverent *Snobbery with Violence: Crime Stories and their Audience* (London: Eyre and Spottiswoode, 1971).

For Burgh Island see *The Great White Palace*, Tony Porter (London: Transworld, 2003).

For the French Riviera see Riviera: *The Rise and Fall of the Côte d'Azur*, Jim Ring, (London: John Murray, 2004) and *Everybody Was So Young: Gerald and Sara Murphy: A Lost Generation Love Story*, Amanda Vaill (Boston: Houghton Mifflin Co, 1998) and *Tender is the Night: A Romance*, F. Scott Fitzgerald, (London: Penguin, 1986).

For the rise of sunbathing, swimming and so on, see above and general seaside histories per chapter one and *Sun, Fun and Crowds: Seaside Holidays Between the Wars*, Steven Braggs and Diane Harris, (Stroud: Tempus, 2000) and *Swimwear in Vogue: since 1910*, Christina Probert (London: Thames and Hudson, 1981).

For the seaside modernism see above and *The Architectural Review*, July 1936, *England's Seaside Resorts*, Allan Brodie and Gary Winter (English Heritage, 2007), *Modernism on Sea: Art and Culture at the British Seaside*, ed. Lara Feigel and Alexandra Harris (Oxford: Peter Lang, 2009), *Seaside Surrealism: Paul Nash in Swanage*, Pennie Denton (Peveril Press, 2002) and *Progress at Pelvis Bay*, Osbert Lancaster (London: John Murray, 1936).

For the Midland Hotel see *The Midland Hotel: Morecambe's White Hope*, Barry Guise and Pam Brook (Preston: Palatine, 2008) and *I Know Where I'm Going: A Guide to Morecambe and Heysham,* Michael Bracewell and Linder (London: Bookworks, 2003).

For Bexhill see *De La Warr Pavilion: The Modernist Masterpiece,* Alastair Fairley (Merrell, 2006), *Erich Mendelsohn, 1887–1953* (London: Modern British Architecture in conjunction with A3 Times, 1987) and *The Story of Bexhill* L.J. Bartley (Bexhill-on-Sea: F.J. Parsons Ltd, 1971).

Chapter Five: Camp It Up

For Billy Butlin and his camps see *The Billy Butlin story: 'A Showman to the End',* Sir Billy Butlin with Peter Dacre (London: Robson, 1982), *The Butlin Story,* Rex North (London: Jarrolds, 1962), *Hello Campers!,* Sue Read with Brian Haynes, Peter Scott (London: Bantam Press, 1986), *A History of the Butlin's Railways,* 2001), *Billy Bunter at Butlin's,* Charles Hamilton (London: Cassell, 1961) and *Our True Intent Is All For Your Delight: The John Hinde Butlin's Photographs,* introduction by Martin Parr, photography by Elmar Ludwig, Edmund Nägle and David Noble (London: Chris Boot, 2002).

For an invaluable overview of the whole phenomena see *Goodnight Campers!: The History of the British Holiday Camp,* Colin Ward and Dennis Hardy (London: Mansell Publishing Ltd, 1986).

For Cunningham's Camp see *Good Clean Fun: The Story of Britain's First Holiday Camp,* Jill Drower (London: Arcardia, 1982).

For the civil service camps see *So Far,* W. J. Brown, (Allen and Unwin: London, 1943).

For Priestley on Blackpool see *English Journey: Being a Rambling but Truthful Account of what One Man Saw and Heard and Felt and Thought During a Journey Through England During the Autumn of the Year 1933,* J.B. Priestley (Harmondsworth: Penguin, 1977).

Chapter Six: The Good Life

Cammaerts' view of England and its relationship to the past is quoted in *The English: A Portrait of a People,* Jeremy Paxman (London: Michael Joseph, 1998).

L. P. Hartley's *The Shrimp and the Anemone* is London: Faber, 2000, originally published: London: Putnam, 1944.

Westward Ho! was A British Travel Association film 1961, directed and photographed by Martin Rolfe.

For Betjeman on the West Country see *Cornwall Illustrated in a Series of Views,* John Betjeman (London: Architectural Press: A Shell Guide, 1933), *Devon,* John Betjeman (London: Architectural Press: A Shell Guide, 1936), *Betjeman's Cornwall,* John Betjeman (London: John Murray, 1988) *Trains and Buttered Toast: Selected Radio Talks,* John Betjeman, ed. Stephen Games (London: John Murray, 2007) and *Betjeman's England,* John Betjeman, ed. Stephen Games (London: John Murray, 2009).

For Du Maurier see *Vanishing Cornwall,* Daphne du Maurier; photographs by Christian Browning (London: V. Gollancz, 1981), *Enchanted Cornwall: Her Pictorial Memoir,* Daphne Du Maurier (London: M.Joseph, 1992) and *Daphne du Maurier Country Martyn Shallcross,* (Bodmin: Bossiney, 1987).

For Wilkie Collins see *Rambles Beyond Railways: or, Notes in Cornwall Taken A-Foot*, Wilkie Collins (London: Bentley, 1851).

Val Denys Baker's radio play is *Cornwall for the Cornish* (St. Ives: Porthmeor Press, 1964) and his survey of the St Ives' scene is *Britain's Art Colony by the Sea* (Ronald,1959).

For St Ives, Wallis et. al. see *Painting the Warmth of the Sun: St Ives Artists, 1939–1975*, Tom Cross (Tiverton: Westcountry, 1995), *Ben Nicholson: The Vicious Circles of his Life and Art*, Sarah Jane Checkland (London: John Murray, 2000) *Alfred Wallis, Christopher Wood, Ben Nicholson: Modern, the Primitive and the Picturesque,* Charles Harrison, Margaret Gardiner (Edinburgh: Scottish Arts Council and the Pier Arts Centre, 1987), *Alfred Wallis: Primitive,* Sven Berlin, (London: Nicholson and Watson, 1949), *Alfred Wallis: Cornish Primitive,* Edwin Mullins (London: Pavilion, 1994), *Alfred Wallis,* Matthew Gale (London: Tate Gallery Publishing, 1998) and *Alfred Wallis, Artist and Mariner,* Robert Jones (Tiverton: Halsgrove, 2001).

Chapter Seven: Fighting on the Beaches

Folk Devils and Moral Panics: The Creation of the Mods and Rockers, Stanley Cohen (Oxford: Martin Robertson, 1980) remains the definitive chronicle of events but for fresher material also see 'Forty years ago pictures of Mods and Rockers shocked polite society. But were they staged by the press?', Robin Summer, *Independent on Sunday,* 4 April 2004.

Quotes from Colin MacInnes are taken from *Absolute Beginners* (London: Allison and Busby, 1980). Also see *England, Half English* Colin MacInnes (London: Hogarth, 1986), c1961 for his non-fiction take on the period's youth styles.

For Mods consult, *Mods!,* Richard Barnes, (London: Plexus 2009), *The Soul Stylists: Six Decades of Modernism from Mods to Casuals,* Paolo Hewitt, (Edinburgh: Mainstream, 2003) and

Howard Baker's novel *Sawdust Caesar* (Edinburgh: Mainstream, 1999).

For Rockers see *Rockers!*, Johnny Stuart (London: Plexus, 1987) and *Bikers: Birth of a Modern-Day Outlaw*, Maz Harris (London: Faber, 1985), the latter is especially good. And for Hell's Angels naturally see Hunter S. Thompson's *Hell's Angels* (London: Penguin, 1967 (1977)).

Quotes from Mick Farren on the Easter weekend are from *Give the Anarchist a Cigarette* (London: Jonathan Cape, 2001).

The sounds of The Who's My Generation and Quadrophenia LPs and the sights of Sidney Furie's film *The Leather Boys* and Franc Roddam's *Quadrophenia* were all in here too somewhere.

Chapter Eight: End of the Pierrot

The figures on retirement trends were taken from 'Retirement property: follow the market,' Caroline McGhie, *Daily Telegraph*, 24 November 2009.

For the historical perspective on coastal retirement see Anthony Hern, *The Seaside Holiday: The History of the English Seaside Resort* (London: Cresset Press, 1967).

The circumstances surrounding the creation of Pinter's *The Birthday Party* are chronicled in *Harold Pinter*, Michael Billington (London: Faber, 2007).

For Dad's Army see *The Complete A–Z of Dad's Army*, Richard Webber (London: Orion, 2000) and for Le Mesurier and Tony Hancock see *Tony Hancock: The Definitive Biography*, John Fisher (London: HarperCollins, 2008) and *Tony Hancock*, Philip Oakes (London: Woburn Press, 1975).

Quotes from Anthony Powell's *The Kindly Ones* are (London: Mandarin, 1991, c1962).

For Aleister Crowley see *The Great Beast: The Life and Magick of Aleister Crowley,* John Symonds (London: Macdonald and Co., 1971), *A Magick Life: The Biography of Aleister Crowley*, Martin Booth (London: Hodder & Stoughton, 2000), *Aleister Crowley: The Beast Demystified*, Roger Hutchinson (Edinburgh: Mainstream, 1998), *Aleister Crowley*, Charles Cammell (London: New English Library, 1969) and, particularly to do with Crowley's time in Hastings, *Remembering Aleister Crowley*, Kenneth Grant (London: Skoob, 1991).

The more recent coastal drug statistics are from 'High Tide', *The Economist,* 30 July 2009. For the history see *Heroin Addiction Care and Control: The British System, 1916–1984* H.B. Spear; edited by Joy Mott (London: DrugScope, 2002) and 'A Lost War', Alan Travis, *The Guardian,* 11 September 2002.

Christie's is again *Evil Under the Sun,* Agatha Christie (London: HarperCollins, 1999, c1941).

Quotes from *The History Man* are Malcolm Bradbury (London: Secker and Warburg, 1975). And Raban's *Coasting* is (London: Collins Harvill, 1986).

For *Howard's Way* see Mathew Sweet's 'What Howard's Way Tells Us About the Eighties' in *Shouting at the Telly*, ed. John Grindrod (London: Faber, 2009) and for Bergerac see my own essay 'Kill the Cops' in the same volume.

For Martin Parr's images of New Brighton see *The Last Resort: Photographs of New Brighton*, Martin Parr, text by Ian Walker (Wallasey: Promenade Press, 1986).

The figures on visitors to seaside resorts are from *The Englishman's Holiday: A Social History*, J. R. Pimlott (London: Faber, 1947).

For an overview of their general problems since the war see *The Rise and Fall of British Coastal Resorts: Cultural and Economic Perspectives*, edited by Gareth Shaw and Allan Williams (London: Mansell, 1997).

And last but by no means least, the superb *I Know Where I'm Going: A Guide to Morecambe and Heysham* by Michael Bracewell and Linder (London: Bookworks, 2003), shaped many of thoughts on the reclaiming of the coasts by artists and the artistically inclined.

Epilogue

The 2006 DVD edition of Franc Roddam's film *Quadrophenia* includes interviews with and commentaries from the director and cast.